LIFE IS A GAME

SHRISH BOHRA

notionpress.com

INDIA · SINGAPORE · MALAYSIA

Contents

Note to the Reader

Dear Reader,

Welcome to *Life is a Game*—a journey through the many dimensions of life, where each experience is a move on the board, and every decision plays a role in shaping your future. This book isn't a guide for winning according to someone else's rules but an invitation to own your game, create your own path, and grow through every challenge and success that life throws at you.

You will explore the complexities of love, emotions, money, and relationships in a way that helps you understand not just how to succeed, but how to thrive. Whether it's learning from heartbreak, mastering your emotions, building financial security, or navigating your passions, each chapter will equip you with the tools to better understand yourself and the world around you.

Remember, life is not just about getting to the end or collecting victories—it's about playing with purpose, embracing the highs and lows, and becoming stronger, wiser, and more resilient with each step. The game is yours to define, and my hope is that through this book, you'll find clarity, motivation, and insight to not just play the game, but to truly *own* it.

Enjoy the journey, and may you embrace the game of life with open arms and an open mind.

Warm regards,
Shrish Bohra

Introduction: Why You Should Read This Book

Life can often feel overwhelming, like a series of unpredictable twists and turns where you're constantly struggling to keep up. At times, you may feel like you're simply a participant, going through the motions, trying to meet the expectations of others. But what if you could see life from a different perspective—a game where every choice, relationship, and challenge present an opportunity for growth and mastery?

That's what this book is about:

Life is a Game isn't about winning in the traditional sense. It's about learning how to navigate life's complexities with the mindset that you can shape your own path, on your own terms. By understanding each key aspect of life—love, emotions, money, and relationships—you can develop the tools to approach life not just as a passive player, but as someone who takes ownership, makes thoughtful decisions, and learns from every experience.

Chapter 1: The Game of Love

Love is one of the most powerful forces in our lives, but it is also one of the most complicated. Whether it's the excitement and heartbreak of romantic relationships, the loyalty and trust of friendships, or the unconditional love of family, understanding how love functions as a game can help you navigate its highs and lows with more clarity and purpose. By seeing love as something that evolves, requires effort, and teaches us valuable lessons, you can approach relationships with a healthier, more balanced mindset.

Chapter 2: The Game of Emotions

Emotions are at the core of every decision we make, but too often, we let them control us instead of mastering them. This chapter will show you how to navigate your emotions like a skilled player, using emotional intelligence to better understand yourself and others. By learning how to balance logic with emotion and manage negative feelings constructively, you can play the game of life with more confidence and control, rather than being swept away by emotional turbulence.

Chapter 3: The Game of Seduction

Seduction isn't just about romantic attraction; it's about confidence, charm, and how you present yourself to the world. This chapter will help you understand the power of attraction in all areas of life, from personal relationships to professional settings. By developing self-confidence, respecting boundaries, and building genuine connections, you can navigate social dynamics with ease and build relationships based on mutual respect and attraction.

Chapter 4: The Game of Money

Money is often a source of stress, yet it's one of the most important elements in life that requires thoughtful strategy. Whether you're saving for the future, managing day-to-day expenses, or investing to build wealth, understanding the game of money is crucial. This chapter will provide you with practical strategies to help you master your financial life—ensuring that you aren't just surviving, but thriving with financial freedom and security.

Chapter 5: The Game of Life

Life, at its core, is the ultimate game. It connects everything else—your relationships, your emotions, and your financial well-being. Understanding the game of life means figuring out what your purpose is, what drives you, and how to overcome the inevitable challenges that will come your way. This chapter will guide you in discovering your passions and navigating life's obstacles, helping you find meaning and direction on your journey.

Final Thoughts

This book is a guide to approaching life with the mindset that every experience is a move in the game, every failure is a lesson, and every success is a stepping stone toward something greater. It's about playing with intention, learning from every challenge, and defining your own path to fulfilment. *Life is a Game* offers the insights you need to start playing life on your own terms—so dive in, and remember, the game is yours to own.

Chapter 1

The Game of Love – Romantic, Parental, and Friendship

Understanding the Game of Love

Love is the most misunderstood force in the world. We grow up with fairy tales, believing that love is simple—a straight path to happiness, where two people meet, fall in love, and live happily ever after. But if you've ever truly loved, you know that's a lie. Love is not a smooth, romanticized journey. It's messy. It's painful. It demands more from you than you ever thought you could give. The truth is, love is a game, and if you don't know how to play, it will tear you apart.

In this chapter, we'll break down the game of love—romantic love, parental love, and friendship. But be warned, you may realize that everything you thought you knew about love was wrong.

1. Love Requires Vulnerability

"To love at all is to be vulnerable.
Love anything and your heart will be
wrung and possibly broken."
— **C.S. Lewis**

Most people think love is about finding someone who completes you, someone who makes you feel safe and whole. But real love? It's not safe at all. Love is stepping into the fire, knowing full well you might get burned. It's standing naked in front of someone emotionally, with no armour, no shield—just you, in all your raw, unfiltered humanity.

And here's the truth no one wants to admit: that's terrifying. Love asks you to hand someone the power to break you completely. It's terrifying because you will get hurt. It's not *if*—it's *when*. That's what love does. It breaks you, because only in the breaking can you really know the depths of what it means to love someone. Vulnerability is the price you pay to feel love's highs and endure its lows.

We guard ourselves from vulnerability because we think it will protect us. But all that does is keep love at a distance. Without vulnerability, you can never fully connect with someone. Love isn't about avoiding pain. It's about risking it all, knowing that the very act of opening up to someone might destroy you—and doing it anyway. Because love without risk, without vulnerability, is no love at all.

2. Love Demands Communication

*"The single biggest problem in communication is the
illusion that it has taken place."*
— **George Bernard Shaw**

Love isn't just a feeling. It's a constant, conscious effort. And the biggest lie we've been sold about love is that it should be easy. That if you love someone enough, they should just know what you need. But here's the hard truth: love without communication is like building a house on sand. It might look fine for a while, but eventually, it collapses.

We get caught in the trap of thinking; *they should understand me. They should know what I need.* But they don't. They can't. No one is a mind reader, and assuming they are is what destroys relationships. Silence kills more love than hate ever could.

When you don't say what's in your heart, resentment grows. You pull away, assuming they don't care, when in reality, they just don't know. You assume your needs don't matter, or worse, that they *should* know without you having to say a word. This is the silent killer of love—expecting someone to meet needs they don't even know exist.

True love isn't in the grand gestures, the romantic dates, or the poetic words. It's in the uncomfortable conversations at midnight, where you say what you really feel, not just what you think they want to hear. It's in telling someone the truth about who you are and what you need, even if it scares you. Because love without communication is just a slow death waiting to happen.

3. Love is a Balancing Act

"In a relationship, it's not about the person you can live with, but the person you can't live without."
— **Anonymous**

They tell you love is about compromise. That's the advice everyone gives— *"relationships are all about give and take."* But no one tells you what happens when you're the only one giving. No one warns you that love can quickly turn into a trap where you lose yourself trying to make the other person happy.

Love is balance. But balance doesn't mean giving up who you are just to keep the peace. Too often, we pour everything we have into someone else, hoping they'll do the same, only to find ourselves depleted, empty, and wondering why we feel so lost. Real love isn't about sacrificing yourself until there's nothing left. It's about both people holding each other up, both people pouring into each other's cup.

You shouldn't have to lose yourself to keep someone else. If the scales are always tipped in their favour, that's not love—that's manipulation, whether intentional or not. And here's the hard truth: if you're constantly the one giving, eventually, you'll burn out. You'll resent them, not because of what they've done, but because of what you've allowed.

Real love means knowing your worth, and making sure that the love you give is returned. You deserve to be loved as much as you love others. Don't settle for a one-sided relationship where you're always the one fighting to make it work. Balance is the key. Without it, love turns toxic.

4. Love Involves Growth

"We are not the same person this year as last; nor are those we love. It is a happy chance if we, changing, continue to love a changed person."
— **W. Somerset Maugham**

We want love to be forever. We want the person we fall in love with to stay the same, to keep loving us in the same way, with the same intensity, as they did in the beginning. But here's the truth: people change. You will change. And love? It has to change, too.

One of the most painful lessons in love is realizing that the person you once knew no longer exists. The person who once made your heart race, the one who felt like your whole world—they will evolve, and so will you. And sometimes, you'll grow together. But sometimes, you'll grow apart. That's the reality no one talks about.

Love isn't about trying to freeze time. It's about growing with the person you love, allowing them to evolve, even if it means they're no longer the person you fell in love with. You have to accept that love will change, and you have to be willing to adapt. The kind of love that lasts isn't stagnant—it's fluid, always changing, always evolving.

If you cling to the past, to the version of someone who no longer exists, you'll end up resenting who they've become. To love truly is to let go of your need to control the outcome. It's allowing yourself and the person you love to grow, even if that means facing the hard truth that you might grow in different directions.

5. Love is Not Always Fair

"Sometimes the person you'd take a bullet
for is the one behind the trigger."
— **Taylor Swift**

Here's the harshest truth about love: it's not fair. It's never been fair. You can love someone with everything you have, and they can still hurt you. They can still betray you, leave you, or break your heart in ways you never imagined. And there's nothing you can do about it.

We're taught that if we love someone enough, if we're good enough, if we give enough, they'll never leave us. But that's not how love works. Love is a gamble. You can give someone your heart, your soul, your entire world—and they can still turn around and crush it. Not because you weren't enough, but because that's how life is sometimes.

And here's the thing: you have to learn to be okay with that. You have to accept that love will hurt you, that people you trust will let you down, that sometimes, no matter how much you love, it won't be enough to make them stay.

But that doesn't mean love isn't worth it. It just means that love is about risk. Every time you open your heart, you're gambling with your happiness. Sometimes, you'll win. And sometimes, you'll lose everything. But in losing, you learn. You learn what you need, what you deserve, and what you will never settle for again.

Love will break you, but it will also teach you how to rise.

6. Why Understanding Love as a Game Matters

Love isn't the fairy tale we've been sold. It's a game. A game where the rules are constantly changing, where there are no guarantees, and where the only certainty is that you'll get hurt. But it's a game worth playing because, in the end, love isn't about winning or losing—it's about learning.

It's about learning that love requires vulnerability, even when it terrifies you. It's about understanding that without communication, love dies in silence. It's about finding balance, so you don't lose yourself while loving someone else. It's about growing together, knowing that love evolves and that you have to evolve with it. And most importantly, it's about accepting that love isn't fair, but it's still the most powerful force in the world.

The game of love isn't one you can master. It's one you experience, one you survive, one that changes you in ways you never thought possible. And that's why it's worth playing.

Romantic Love – The game of Joy and the Risk

Life is a complex game, but there's no part of it more profound, more exhilarating, or more devastating than love—especially romantic love. We're taught to believe that love is a magical feeling, a fairy tale where everything falls into place, and life just works out when you meet "the one." But the reality is, love isn't a story with a guaranteed happy ending. It's a game, one that requires risk, vulnerability, and an understanding that you may not always come out as the winner. Sometimes, love brings you to your knees, leaving you shattered. But the beauty of this game is that you always have the chance to get up and play again.

Romantic love is powerful, but it's fragile. It's a thrilling adventure, but it's also a dangerous game that can turn your world upside down. The highs are unimaginable, and the lows can be earth-shattering. To truly understand love—and to play this game well—you need to be willing to experience both the joy and the heartbreak, because one cannot exist without the other.

1. The Power of True Connection

Romantic love begins with a spark—an undeniable connection. It's that moment when you lock eyes with someone across the room and feel like you've known them your entire life. The world fades away, and suddenly, it's just the two of you. The rush of emotions is intoxicating. In those first moments, you feel invincible, like nothing could ever break this bond. But here's the truth: love is not about that initial connection. Love is about what you do with that connection once the honeymoon phase fades away.

> *"Love is composed of a single soul inhabiting two bodies." – Aristotle*

In today's world, it's easy to confuse attraction with love. We live in a culture of instant gratification, where everything is replaceable, including people. The thrill of newness can blind us to the deeper aspects of love, and many of us move on when the excitement fades, chasing that initial high again and again. But that's not how you win the game of love. That's how you lose it.

True connection takes time. It takes effort, vulnerability, and patience. It's not just about the good times, the laughter, and the moments of passion. It's about showing up for each other when things get tough. It's about staying even when the excitement has worn off. It's about committing to the other person, flaws and all, and building something real.

> *"Real love isn't just about how you feel, it's about how you make the other person feel."*
> *– Unknown*

We often think that love is about finding the perfect person, but that's not the game we're playing. The real game is about growing with someone, creating a bond that goes beyond chemistry. It's about being each other's support system, best friend, and partner in life. If we focus only on the initial connection, we'll miss out on the depth that comes with true, lasting love.

2. The Destruction of Betrayal

There's nothing more painful in the game of love than betrayal. It's the cruellest move, one that can ruin everything you've built together. When someone you love cheats on you, it's more than just a breach of trust—it's a soul-deep wound that can shatter your heart into a million pieces. Betrayal takes everything beautiful about love and turns it into a nightmare. It's a betrayal not just of the relationship, but of your faith in love itself.

"The saddest thing about betrayal is that it never comes from your enemies." – Unknown

When you trust someone enough to open your heart to them, you're giving them the most vulnerable part of yourself. You're saying, "Here I am, flaws and all, take care of me." But when that trust is broken, it feels like the ground has been ripped out from under you. Betrayal makes you question everything—your worth, your choices, and whether love is even real. It leaves scars that may never fully heal.

In the game of love, cheating isn't just a misstep—it's a fatal error. When you cheat, you're not just hurting the other person; you're breaking the rules of the game. You're saying, "I don't care about this relationship, about you, or about the trust we've built." And the pain that comes from that betrayal can be unbearable.

"Betrayal is the only truth that sticks." – Arthur Miller

Cheating isn't just about the act itself; it's about what it represents—the lies, the deceit, the emotional manipulation. It's the realization that the person you thought had your back was playing for themselves all along. And that can destroy not just the relationship, but the person on the receiving end.

3. Healing From Betrayal: A Long, Painful Road

When someone you love betrays you, it feels like the end of the game. It feels like you've lost, like there's no point in even trying anymore. The pain is all-consuming, and it can make you want to close off your heart forever. But the game of life, the game of love, isn't over just because you've been hurt. The beauty of this game is that you always have the chance to start again.

> *"What hurts more, the pain of letting go or the pain of holding on?"*

Healing from betrayal is a long and painful road. There are days when the sadness will feel too heavy to bear, when the thought of trusting someone again seems impossible. But healing is not about erasing the pain; it's about learning to live with it. It's about accepting that, yes, you were hurt, but that doesn't mean you'll never find love again.

In the game of love, healing is one of the most important skills you can learn. It's about resilience, about picking yourself up after you've been knocked down. It's about refusing to let someone else's betrayal define you or your future. The scars from betrayal may never fully disappear, but they don't have to control you. They can become a reminder of your strength, of your ability to survive even the darkest moments.

To truly own the game of love, you have to learn to forgive—not just the person who hurt you, but yourself. Forgive yourself for loving someone who didn't deserve you. Forgive yourself for trusting, for believing in love. Because love isn't the enemy here—betrayal is. And while betrayal can break your heart, it can never break your spirit unless you let it.

4. What We Can Do to Make Love Real Again

In today's world, love often feels like a game of short-term gratification, where people are easily discarded, and relationships are shallow. But if we want to make love real again, we have to start playing the game differently. We need to stop treating love as something that's disposable and start seeing it for what it really is—a lifelong commitment to another person, filled with both joy and pain, but always worth the effort.

To make love real again, we need to go back to the basics. First, we need to value loyalty. In a world where cheating has become normalized, we need to remember that loyalty is the foundation of any real relationship. Loyalty means showing up for each other, day after day, no matter what. It means choosing your partner, not just when it's easy, but when it's hard. Loyalty is what keeps love alive when the excitement fades.

"Loyalty is the strongest glue which makes a relatio nship last for a lifetime." – Mario Puzo

Second, we need to communicate more openly. Love isn't just about grand gestures and romantic dates—it's about the quiet moments of understanding. It's about talking through your fears, your insecurities, and your hopes for the future. In a world filled with distractions, we often forget to truly listen to the people we love. But communication is the lifeblood of any relationship. Without it, love withers and dies.

"The most important thing in communication is hearing what isn't said." – Peter Drucker

Third, we need to be patient. Love isn't always exciting. It's not always passionate. Sometimes, love is mundane. It's waking up next to the same person every day, choosing to love them even when they annoy you, even when you're tired, even when you're not in the mood. Love is a choice, and that choice requires patience. It's about believing that the long game is worth it, that the moments of boredom or frustration are just part of the journey.

And finally, we need to stop running away from love when it gets hard. In today's world, it's so easy to leave when things get tough. We've been conditioned to believe that there's always someone better out there, always a better relationship waiting around the corner. But the truth is, love is hard. It's messy, and it's complicated, and sometimes it feels impossible. But that's what makes it worth fighting for. The people who win at the game of love are the ones who stay, who fight through the tough times, who refuse to give up on the people they love.

5. The Power of Staying

Staying in love is a revolutionary act. In a culture that glorifies instant gratification, staying requires a level of commitment that many people are unwilling to give. But staying is the only way to truly own the game of love. It's easy to walk away when things get hard, but the real challenge—the real reward—comes from staying. Staying means choosing to love someone through the hard times, the boring times, the times when you feel disconnected or frustrated.

> *"It's not about how long you've been together, it's about how much you've been through together." – Unknown*

Staying isn't about settling. It's about believing in the power of love, even when it doesn't feel magical or exciting. It's about recognizing that love is a marathon, not a sprint, and that the people who make it to the finish line are the ones who keep showing up, day after day, year after year.

To stay in love is to understand that love is not about finding the perfect person. It's about building a life with someone, brick by brick, even when some of those bricks are cracked or broken. It's about creating a foundation that's strong enough to withstand the storms of life, the heartbreaks, the betrayals, and the disappointments.

And here's the truth: staying is hard. It's messy, and it's not always rewarding in the short term. But staying is how you win the game. It's how you create something lasting, something real, something that will stand the test of time. Staying is an act of defiance in a world that tells us to move on, to find something new, to never settle. Staying says, "I believe in love, and I'm willing to fight for it."

6. Conclusion: Owning the Game of Romantic Love

Romantic love is one of the most complex, challenging, and rewarding parts of life's game. To truly own it, you need to be willing to play with both your heart and your mind. You need to understand the risks, the rewards, and the responsibilities that come with loving someone. Love isn't about winning or losing—it's about growth, connection, and the willingness to keep playing, even when the odds are against you.

In a world where love is often treated like a game of chance, you have the power to own it by being intentional, honest, and committed. Betrayal may knock you down, but it's your resilience, your ability to stay, and your understanding of what real love requires that will allow you to rise again. Love is the ultimate game, and the only way to truly win is to own every part of it—the joy, the pain, the risks, and the rewards.

> *"To love and be loved is to feel*
> *the sun from both sides."*
> *– David Viscott*

By embracing the game of love with all its complexities, you set yourself up to experience the most profound and enduring connection of all. And that, in the end, is what makes the game worth playing.

Friendship: Trust and Betrayal

Friendship is one of the most powerful and essential bonds we experience in life. It is the foundation upon which we build trust, share joy, and find comfort in moments of despair. A true friend offers not only companionship but also the emotional support that allows us to navigate the various challenges life throws our way. The game of friendship, much like love, requires loyalty, trust, and effort to build a connection that stands the test of time. However, just as friendships can be the most rewarding of all relationships, they can also be the most devastating when they fall apart. Betrayal in friendship cuts deeper than we often expect, leaving scars that can last a lifetime.

1. The Power of a True Friendship: Strength in Unity

At the core of every deep and meaningful friendship is trust, a bond that allows two individuals to rely on one another without fear of judgment or abandonment. True friends are the ones who stand by your side when life gets difficult, who listen without interrupting, and who offer a shoulder to cry on when you need it most. They are the ones who share in your joy when you succeed and who lift you up when you feel defeated. In essence, true friends are the family we choose for ourselves.

"A friend is someone who knows all about you and still loves you." – Elbert Hubbard

A good friendship strengthens you. It offers a sense of belonging, purpose, and understanding. When life becomes overwhelming, a trusted friend can provide perspective and guidance that helps you move forward. They know your flaws but accept them, supporting you through both your triumphs and your failures. In many ways, they act as a mirror, reflecting not just your strengths but also your weaknesses, pushing you to become the best version of yourself.

In a game as complex as life, having a true friend by your side is invaluable. They are your teammates, helping you navigate the unpredictable twists and turns. Whether it's dealing with heartbreak, financial stress, or the loss of a loved one, a good friend becomes your sanctuary, a safe space where you can express your emotions without fear of ridicule or rejection.

"Friendship isn't about whom you've known the longest, it's about who came and never left your side." – Unknown

2. The Destructive Force of a Toxic Friendship

While the joy of a deep friendship can lift you to new heights, the pain of a toxic friendship can bring you crashing down. The betrayal of a friend can leave wounds that are often more painful than those inflicted by romantic partners or family members. Friends are the people we trust with our most vulnerable selves, and when that trust is broken, it feels like a betrayal of the deepest kind.

> *"The worst pain in the world goes beyond the physical. Even further beyond any other emotional pain one can feel. It is the betrayal of a friend."*
> *– Heather Brewer*

A toxic friendship often begins with subtle signs—constant criticism, lack of support, manipulation, or jealousy. Over time, these behaviours begin to erode your self-esteem and sense of security. Unlike a healthy friendship, which is based on mutual respect and care, a toxic friend will use your vulnerabilities against you, twisting the relationship into something harmful and destructive. The effects of such a friendship can be devastating. It can make you question your self-worth, damage your trust in others, and leave you feeling isolated and alone.

Toxic friendships often thrive on power imbalances, where one person dominates and the other is left feeling undervalued and unheard. These relationships are often one-sided, with one friend constantly giving while the other takes. This dynamic can wear you down emotionally, leaving you drained and unfulfilled.

> *"Some people aren't loyal to you; they are loyal to their need of you. Once their needs change, so does their loyalty." – Unknown*

In the game of friendship, a toxic relationship can make you feel like you're always losing. No matter how much effort you put in, no matter how much you care, it never seems to be enough. The pain of betrayal from a friend can linger long after the friendship has ended, making it difficult to trust others or even yourself.

3. The Emotional Bonds of Friendship: A Lifeline in Dark Times

When we think about the most important relationships in our lives, romantic partners and family often come to mind first. But friendship, too, is a deep emotional bond that shapes who we are. In fact, some of the most emotionally fulfilling moments in life come from friendships. There's something unique about the bond between friends—a mutual understanding that doesn't require the same commitments as romantic relationships, yet can often feel just as profound.

The emotional bond between friends is a lifeline, especially during difficult times. Life is unpredictable, filled with hardships, stress, and loss. In these moments, it's our friends who help us survive. They are the ones we call late at night when our thoughts are too heavy to carry alone, the ones who understand our pain without needing an explanation.

> *"A real friend is one who walks in*
> *when the rest of the world walks out."*
> *— Walter Winchell*

Good friends help you carry your burdens. They may not always have the answers, but their presence alone can make even the darkest days seem a little brighter. Through every high and low, they remind you that you are not alone, that someone sees you, understands you, and cares for you.

When a friendship is built on such a strong emotional foundation, it becomes a source of strength. You feel empowered, knowing that no matter what life throws your way, there is someone who has your back. This bond is more than just companionship—it's a deep emotional connection that makes you feel understood, accepted, and loved.

> *"There is nothing on this earth more to*
> *be prized than true friendship."*
> *— Thomas Aquinas*

4. The Joy of Loyalty: The Ultimate Gift of Friendship

Loyalty is the cornerstone of any strong friendship. It's the quiet assurance that no matter what happens, your friend will be there for you. In a world where relationships can often feel fragile, loyalty in friendship is a precious gift. It is a promise that, even when times get tough, even when misunderstandings arise or life pulls you in different directions, your friendship will remain intact.

> *"A friend is someone who can see the truth and pain in you even when you are fooling everyone else."*

Loyalty doesn't mean never having disagreements. In fact, some of the strongest friendships are those where differences are celebrated, and conflicts are handled with respect. Loyalty means that even in moments of disagreement, your friend remains by your side, choosing the friendship over the need to be right. It means that when life gets complicated, they don't walk away—they stay, they listen, and they work through the rough patches with you.

The joy of a loyal friendship is knowing that you have a partner in life, someone who will support you, cheer for you, and defend you when necessary. A loyal friend becomes your confidant, someone you can trust with your secrets, fears, and dreams without the fear of judgment or betrayal.

> *"True friends are never apart, maybe in distance but never in heart." – Helen Keller*

In the game of life, a loyal friend is your greatest ally. They help you navigate through the toughest obstacles, celebrate your victories, and offer comfort in your defeats. They become a source of strength, reminding you that, no matter what, you are not alone.

5. The Devastation of Betrayal: A Shattered Bond

Betrayal by a friend is one of the most painful experiences in life. It's a breaking of trust, a violation of the very foundation upon which the friendship was built. When a friend betrays you, it feels like a part of your soul has been torn away. It's a deeply personal wound, one that cuts to the core of who you are.

"It is easier to forgive an enemy than to forgive a friend." – William Blake

The devastation of betrayal in friendship can come in many forms: lies, manipulation, gossip, or even abandonment. The betrayal may not be immediately obvious, but it slowly erodes the trust that once held the relationship together. And once that trust is broken, it is difficult—if not impossible—to rebuild.

Betrayal in friendship often leads to feelings of isolation and loneliness. The person you once trusted with your deepest fears and dreams has turned against you, leaving you vulnerable and hurt. It makes you question your judgment, your ability to trust others, and your own self-worth.

"False friends are like shadows: they follow you in the sun but leave you in the dark." – Unknown

The emotional impact of betrayal is profound. It can lead to anxiety, depression, and a deep sense of loss. The end of a friendship is like the end of a chapter in your life—a chapter that, despite its pain, shaped who you are.

6. Rebuilding After Betrayal: Healing and Moving Forward

Healing from a broken friendship is not easy. It takes time, introspection, and a willingness to confront the pain head-on. But in the process of healing, we often learn some of the most important lessons in life.

"Sometimes, you have to give up on people.
Not because you don't care, but because they don't."
– Unknown

First, it's important to recognize that not all friendships are meant to last forever. Some are meant to teach us lessons, to help us grow, and then to fade away. This doesn't make the pain of betrayal any less real, but it does offer a sense of closure. The game of friendship, like the game of life, is not about winning or losing—it's about growing, learning, and evolving.

In the aftermath of betrayal, it's essential to allow yourself time to grieve the loss. It's okay to feel hurt, angry, or confused. These emotions are a natural part of the healing process. But eventually, you must find a way to let go of the pain and move forward.

"The only way to have a friend is to be one."
– Ralph Waldo Emerson

Rebuilding trust in others can be difficult after experiencing betrayal, but it's important to remember that not all friendships will end in heartache. There are people out there who will treat you with the respect and loyalty you deserve. Trusting again is a risk, but it's a risk worth taking.

7. The Importance of Choosing the Right Friends

In life's game, the people you choose to surround yourself with have a profound impact on your happiness, success, and overall well-being. A good friend will support you, challenge you, and help you grow. A bad friend, on the other hand, can drain your energy, manipulate you, and lead you down the wrong path.

Choosing the right friends is one of the most important decisions you will make in life. It's important to be discerning, to choose people who add value to your life rather than take away from it. A true friend will respect your boundaries, celebrate your successes, and stand by you in your failures. They will make you feel heard, seen, and valued.

> *"You don't need a lot of friends, just the right ones."*
> *– Unknown*

In the game of friendship, quality always trumps quantity. A small circle of loyal, trustworthy friends is far more valuable than a large group of acquaintances who don't truly care about you. By surrounding yourself with the right people, you set yourself up for success, both emotionally and in the larger game of life.

8. Conclusion: Owning the Game of Friendship

Friendship is one of the most beautiful and complex parts of life. It requires trust, loyalty, and effort to build, but the rewards are immeasurable. A true friend will be there for you through thick and thin, offering support, love, and companionship. But friendship, like all relationships, is not without its risks. Betrayal can leave lasting scars, but it also offers valuable lessons about trust, loyalty, and resilience.

To own the game of friendship, you must be willing to invest in the people who matter, let go of those who don't, and always stay true to yourself. A good friendship can lift you to new heights, while a toxic one can bring you down. Choose your friends wisely, nurture the relationships that bring you joy, and never be afraid to walk away from those that cause you pain.

In the end, the game of friendship is not about having the most friends, but about having the right ones. By surrounding yourself with people who love and support you, you can navigate the ups and downs of life with confidence, knowing that you are never alone.

"Friendship is the only cement that will ever hold the world together." – Woodrow Wilson

And that's the key to owning the game of friendship—understanding that the bonds you build with others have the power to shape your life in ways that no other relationship can. True friends are the ones who help you win, not by playing for you, but by standing beside you as you play your own game.

Parental Love – The Unbreakable Bond of Care and Guidance

Parental love is one of the most profound and enduring relationships we experience in life. Whether it's your biological parents, adoptive parents, guardians, or anyone who has taken on the role of raising and protecting you, the bond between a child and their caretaker is one that shapes your existence in ways you may never fully understand.

This relationship is often misunderstood, underappreciated, or taken for granted—especially when we're young and striving for independence. But as we grow, we begin to see how much of who we are is shaped by the love, sacrifice, and support of the people who stood behind us through every high and low. Parental love is not just about provision or discipline; it's a deep, emotional connection that transcends all logic. It is unconditional, patient, and enduring, even in the face of conflict or distance.

In the game of life, our relationship with our parents or guardians is not just another chapter—it's the foundation. The values we carry, the choices we make, and the way we see the world are all influenced by the people who nurtured us. And yet, the challenge of this relationship lies in its complexity—where misunderstandings, generational gaps, and evolving roles can strain the bond. However, this connection remains one of the most important pillars in our lives, something we often only fully appreciate when we face loss or regret.

`Let's dive deeper into why this relationship is irreplaceable and why, no matter how far we drift, spending time with those who have cared for us is one of the most important things we can do.

1. The Unseen Sacrifices: Love Without Conditions

"Parental love is the only love that is truly selfless, unconditional, and forgiving."
– Dr. T.P. Chia

Behind every parent or guardian stands a series of sacrifices—many of which we may never fully comprehend. These sacrifices are rarely spoken about because they're not given to be noticed. They are made quietly, in the background, as part of the unspoken contract of unconditional love.

As children, we often take these acts for granted. We don't think twice about the nights our mother stayed up late, worried about us, or the way our father worked overtime to make sure we had everything we needed. We don't see the quiet pain they carry when they watch us struggle, knowing they can't protect us from every hurt in the world. Nor do we realize how much of their own dreams they may have put aside to ensure we had the best opportunities.

This sacrifice isn't limited to biological parents. It's in the heart of every grandparent who steps in, every aunt or uncle who takes on the role of caretaker, every guardian who loves you as their own. The sacrifice is universal, and so is the love.

In a world where relationships are often transactional, where people give in order to receive something in return, parental love stands as a stark contrast. They don't love us because we'll pay them back one day or because they expect anything from us. Their love exists solely for our benefit, and it doesn't waver, even when we push them away.

2. The Importance of Time: Giving Back to Those Who Gave Us Everything

"Your parents, they give you your life, but then they try to give you their life." – Chuck Palahniuk

As children, our lives revolve around our parents or guardians. They are our protectors, providers, and first teachers. But as we grow older, we often drift away, absorbed in our own lives and the pursuit of independence. The demands of adulthood—work, relationships, social life—often pull us away from those who raised us. And while this is a natural part of growing up, it's important to remember that time is fleeting, and so are the people we love.

Time spent with your parents or guardians is not just about being physically present. It's about sharing memories, listening to their stories, and understanding the people they are outside of their roles as caregivers. It's about recognizing that while they will always be there for you, they also have dreams, fears, and needs of their own.

Too often, we assume that our parents or guardians will always be there. But life is unpredictable, and moments can slip away before we realize their importance. There's a special kind of heartbreak that comes from realizing, too late, that you didn't spend enough time with the people who mattered most. The regret of not having asked them more about their lives, of not having said "I love you" enough, or of not having been there when they needed you, is a weight that's hard to bear.

Here's a story to illustrate the significance of this bond and the irreplaceable moments we sometimes overlook:

The Story of Mia and Her Father:
A Tale of Lost Paths and Unseen Love

Mia was raised by her father, Daniel, in a small, close-knit town. Her mother had passed away when she was just three years old, leaving Daniel to raise Mia alone. He did everything he could to give her a stable and loving home. A mechanic by trade, Daniel worked long hours, often late into the night, but he always made time for Mia. He was at every parent-teacher conference, every dance recital, and every birthday party. Mia was the light of his life, and he did everything to make sure she never felt the absence of her mother.

Mia was a bright and promising young girl. In high school, she excelled academically and was loved by her friends and teachers. Everyone in the town saw Mia as Daniel's pride and joy. She was kind, respectful, and always smiling. Daniel had high hopes for her future, and when Mia got accepted into a prestigious university far from home, he couldn't have been prouder.

"Make me proud, Mia," he told her with tears in his eyes the day she left for college. "You're going to do great things."

Mia hugged her father tightly, promising him she would make him proud. She knew how much he had sacrificed for her—working late nights, never spending money on himself, just so she could have everything she needed. She left home with a heart full of gratitude and a determination to succeed.

But life at university was nothing like the quiet life she had known at home.

The Temptations of a New Life

At first, Mia stuck to her studies. She called her father every evening, updating him on her classes, telling him how much she missed him. But slowly, things began to change. She started making new friends, friends who introduced her to a lifestyle she had never experienced before.

At first, it was harmless—just a drink here and there, a party on the weekends. Mia felt alive, free, and exhilarated by the new world she had stepped into. No one knew her as Daniel's quiet, obedient daughter here. She could be whoever she wanted to be.

The drinking quickly turned from weekends to weekdays. Mia began to skip classes, choosing instead to go out with her new friends. What started as harmless fun quickly spiraled into a cycle of clubbing, drinking, and partying every night. She found herself smoking cigarettes, something she never imagined she would do, and eventually, she started experimenting with drugs.

Her grades plummeted, but Mia didn't care. The thrill of her new lifestyle consumed her. She was constantly chasing the next high, the next party, the next moment of temporary escape. Her phone calls to her father became less frequent. When she did speak to him, she lied. She told him everything was fine, that she was doing well in her classes, that she had made good friends. She told him the university was hard, but she was managing.

Daniel, ever the proud father, believed her. He never doubted Mia's words. Why would he? She had always been so responsible, so trustworthy. He couldn't imagine his daughter was leading a life so far from the one he had raised her to live.

The Downward Spiral

Mia's life began to spiral out of control. She no longer cared about her studies or her future. She partied until the early hours of the morning, slept with different guys she barely knew, and used drugs to keep herself going. Her once bright future seemed to fade with every passing day.

But she kept lying to her father.

Every time Daniel called, Mia would put on her best voice, telling him she was studying hard, that everything was great, and that she was staying focused on her goals. Daniel would often ask when she would come home to visit. He missed her terribly, but Mia always found excuses. She told him she was too busy, that there were too many assignments, or that she was volunteering at school.

"I'm so proud of you, Mia," Daniel would say. "You're doing great things."

And every time he said those words, a pang of guilt would twist in Mia's stomach, but she pushed it away, choosing instead to drown it in another drink, another hit, another night out. The truth was too ugly to face, and the lies were easier to maintain.

But eventually, the weight of her choices caught up with her.

The Fall

One night, after a particularly wild party, Mia found herself alone in her apartment, staring at her reflection in the bathroom mirror. Her face was gaunt, her eyes bloodshot. She barely recognized herself anymore. Her grades had hit rock bottom, she was on the verge of being expelled, and the friends she had partied with had started to disappear as well.

As she looked at herself, the image of her father flashed in her mind—his kind eyes, his tired hands, his unwavering love. She thought about all the sacrifices he had made for her, all the times he had put her first, all the trust he had placed in her. And here she was, wasting everything he had worked so hard to give her.

For the first time in months, Mia felt the weight of her guilt. She had lied to her father, she had betrayed his trust, and she had become someone she didn't even recognize. Tears streamed down her face as she sank to the floor, sobbing uncontrollably.

She realized then that she had been running from herself, running from the pain of losing her mother, running from the responsibility of living up to her father's expectations. And in doing so, she had lost everything that truly mattered.

The Call Home

The next day, Mia did something she hadn't done in months—she called her father.

"Dad," she said, her voice shaky and weak.

"Mia! It's so good to hear from you," Daniel said, his voice filled with warmth. "How's everything going? I've been missing you."

Mia choked on her words, the guilt flooding her chest. "Dad, I'm not doing well," she finally admitted. "I've been lying to you. I've messed up... really badly."

There was a long pause on the other end of the line, and Mia braced herself for the disappointment she knew she deserved.

"Mia," Daniel said softly, "whatever it is, we'll get through it. You're my daughter, and I love you. No matter what."

And that was it. No anger, no yelling, no shaming. Just love. Unconditional, unwavering love.

Mia broke down, confessing everything to her father—the drugs, the drinking, the failing grades, the lies. She told him how she had been wasting her life, how she had lost sight of everything that mattered, how she had let him down.

But Daniel didn't focus on what she had done wrong. Instead, he focused on how to help her move forward. He reminded her that she was not alone, that no mistake was too big to fix, and that he would always be there for her, no matter what.

The Road to Redemption

Mia returned home shortly after that phone call. Her father welcomed her with open arms, never once holding her past against her. Together, they worked through her pain, her guilt, and her fear. Mia slowly rebuilt her life, with her father's love and support guiding her every step of the way.

She enrolled in therapy, quit her destructive habits, and started taking small steps toward healing. It wasn't easy, and there were moments when Mia felt like giving up. But every time she stumbled, Daniel was there to catch her, just as he had been her whole life.

It took time, but Mia eventually found her way back to herself. She re-enrolled in school, surrounded herself with healthier friends, and began to take responsibility for her actions. And through it all, her father remained her rock, his love the steady force that helped her rise from the ashes of her mistakes.

The Lesson

Mia's story is one of countless others. So many young people leave home, eager to experience freedom, only to lose themselves in the temptations of a life without boundaries. They lie to their parents, thinking they're protecting them from the truth, not realizing that the lies they tell are slowly destroying the trust and love that their parents have placed in them.

But the lesson Mia learned is one that we all must face at some point in our lives: no matter how far we stray, no matter how badly we mess up, the people who love us the most are often the ones who are willing to forgive us, to help us rebuild, and to stand by us when no one else will.

Parents, guardians, and those who care for us give their lives to ensure we have the chance to live ours. They trust us to make the right choices, to live up to our potential, and to carry their love with us wherever we go. But when we betray that trust, when we take their love for granted, we not only hurt them—we hurt ourselves.

The Game of Life and Love

In the game of life, our relationship with our parents or guardians is the foundation upon which everything else is built. Their love is not something to be taken lightly or to be thrown away in the pursuit of fleeting pleasures. It's a love that endures, even when we fall, even when we make mistakes, even when we lie.

But the real game—the game of love—is about owning up to those mistakes, facing the consequences of our actions, and working to rebuild the trust we've lost. It's about understanding that the people who have loved us from the beginning deserve our honesty, our time, and our respect.

Mia's story is a reminder that it's never too late to turn things around. It's never too late to call home, to ask for help, to admit that we've made mistakes. And it's never too late to start living a life that honors the love and sacrifices of the people who raised us.

So, if you're reading this and you've been hiding the truth from the people who love you, ask yourself: Is it worth it? Are the lies, the parties, the mistakes worth the pain and the guilt? Or is it time to face the truth, to come home, and to start living a life that reflects the love you've been given?

Because in the end, the real game of life isn't about how far you can run—it's about how well you can find your way back.

3. Parental Love: The Invisible Strength Behind Every Success

"A parent's love is whole, no matter
how many times divided."
– Robert Brault

Behind every success story is someone who believed in you, supported you, and gave you the strength to keep going when times were tough. For many of us, that person is our parent or guardian. Their love is the silent force that propels us forward, even when we don't realize it.

When you reflect on your life, think about all the times you've stumbled, felt lost, or doubted yourself. Who was there to pick you up? Who believed in you when you didn't believe in yourself? Who gave you the courage to chase your dreams, even when the world seemed to be against you?

Parental love is the invisible safety net that catches us when we fall. It's the unwavering support that allows us to take risks, knowing that someone will be there to help us if we fail. This kind of love is rare and irreplaceable, and it's something we should never take for granted.

4. The Role Reversal: When the Child Becomes the Caregiver

"We never know the love of a parent until we become parents ourselves." – Henry Ward Beecher

As we grow older, the roles between parent and child often begin to shift. The people who once cared for us, protected us, and guided us through life may become the ones who need our care and support. This transition can be difficult to navigate, both emotionally and practically, but it is a natural part of life.

Caring for an aging parent or guardian is one of the most profound acts of love we can give. It's a way of honouring the sacrifices they made for us and showing them that their love did not go unnoticed. It's a way of giving back, of saying, "I see you. I appreciate you. And now it's my turn to take care of you."

This role reversal can be challenging. Watching someone who was once strong and capable become vulnerable can be heartbreaking. But it also offers an opportunity to deepen the bond between parent and child. It allows us to see our parents as more than just caregivers, but as people with their own fears, dreams, and struggles.

5. Conclusion: The Game of Love Through a Parent's Eyes

In the game of life, parental love is the foundation upon which everything else is built. It's the love that teaches us how to love, how to trust, and how to forgive. It's the love that gives us the strength to face life's challenges and the courage to chase our dreams.

But like any game, the relationship between parent and child is not without its challenges. There will be misunderstandings, conflicts, and moments of distance. But through it all, the bond remains. Because at the core of every parental relationship is a love that transcends time, space, and even death.

So, if you're reading this, take a moment to reflect on the people who raised you. Whether it's your biological parents, adoptive parents, grandparents, or guardians, they have played a pivotal role in shaping who you are. They have loved you in ways you may never fully understand, and they deserve your time, your appreciation, and your love in return.

The game of life is long and unpredictable, but one thing is certain: the love of a parent is a gift that should never be taken for granted.

Conquering the Game of Love:

The Game of Love is one of the most profound, yet challenging aspects of life. It isn't about mastering others, but about mastering yourself within the relationships you hold. Romantic love, friendships, and parental bonds make up the core elements of this game. Each form of love has its own rules, lessons, and emotional depths, but they all share one common truth: love is about connection, vulnerability, and the courage to show up fully for another person, even when it's hard. To truly conquer the game of love, it's essential to understand that winning is not about perfection, but about resilience, growth, and emotional investment.

1. Romantic Love: Healing Through Authenticity and Empathy

Romantic love often feels like the most emotionally intense form of connection. It involves both passion and vulnerability, and when it goes wrong, it can leave lasting scars. But the game of love isn't just about finding that perfect romantic partner; it's about building and maintaining a deep connection despite the imperfections on both sides.

Real Love Demands Authenticity

In romantic relationships, authenticity is the foundation. It can be tempting to present an idealized version of yourself—someone who seems flawless or perfectly suited for your partner's expectations. However, a love built on pretense will eventually crumble. True love means letting down your guard, showing your partner who you really are, and accepting who they truly are in return.

Imagine a couple who met in a whirlwind of passion, each seeing only the best version of the other. Over time, the cracks in their façades start to show. They start arguing over small things, pointing out flaws and imperfections. Instead of hiding behind masks, they could choose to embrace vulnerability. Saying, "This is who I really am, scars and all," opens the door to deeper intimacy. When both people are willing to be real, love stops being a shallow game of appearances and turns into something much more profound.

Empathy as the Glue in Romantic Relationships

Love isn't just about giving; it's also about understanding. Empathy is the key to navigating difficult times in any romantic relationship. Putting yourself in your partner's shoes—truly feeling what they're feeling—creates an emotional bond that transcends the temporary issues or frustrations you might face.

For those who have faced infidelity, emotional distance, or conflict, empathy is the pathway to healing. If you're the one who's been hurt, it might feel impossible to understand how your partner could betray your trust. But empathy doesn't mean excusing behaviour—it means understanding the emotions and triggers behind it, which allows you to rebuild from a place of compassion, rather than anger.

2. Friendship: The Importance of Trust and Loyalty

Friendships, like romantic relationships, play an integral role in our lives. The connection you have with your closest friends often serves as a lifeline, providing emotional support, companionship, and a sense of belonging. But just like romantic love, friendship can be fragile if not cared for properly.

True Friendship is Built on Trust

Trust is the backbone of any friendship. It allows for vulnerability, openness, and emotional support. When trust is broken—whether by betrayal, dishonesty, or neglect—the friendship can falter. But trust can be rebuilt, and with effort, even stronger friendships can emerge from the pain.

Take, for example, two best friends who have drifted apart. Maybe one friend shared a secret, or one simply stopped showing up when the other needed them most. Rebuilding that trust means having a heart-to-heart conversation, where both parties acknowledge the hurt and express their commitment to repairing the relationship. Trust isn't rebuilt overnight, but through small, consistent actions that prove loyalty.

The Impact of Loyalty and Reliability

In friendship, loyalty isn't just about sticking around during the good times; it's about being there through life's messiness. A loyal friend doesn't run away when things get tough; they show up even when it's inconvenient or difficult. And in the game of life, this kind of loyalty is invaluable.

For those who have lost friends due to misunderstandings or conflicts, the way back is through reliability. If you've been unreliable or inconsistent, now is the time to prove that you are someone who can be counted on. By showing up regularly, keeping your word, and being emotionally available, you demonstrate that you're committed to making the friendship last.

3. Parental Love: The Steadfast Anchor in the Storm

Parental love, whether from biological parents, guardians, or anyone who has been a steady figure in your life, forms the emotional core of our early experiences with love. This love is often taken for granted, especially as we grow older and become more independent. However, this bond is one of the most critical aspects of love to nurture, because it offers lessons in sacrifice, endurance, and unconditional support.

The Unseen Sacrifices of Parental Love

Parents or guardians often make sacrifices that their children may never fully understand. These sacrifices can be emotional, financial, and even personal. Whether it's a father working long hours to provide for his family or a guardian quietly putting their dreams aside to support a child's future, these acts of love are often unseen and unappreciated. Yet, they form the foundation of a child's life and well-being.

For those who may feel distant from their parents, taking the time to reflect on these sacrifices can be a humbling and emotional experience. It's easy to focus on what our parents didn't do right or how they failed us, but it's equally important to recognize the incredible things they did without ever expecting recognition. Realizing this can inspire a deeper connection and a desire to give back in ways that honour their efforts.

Nurturing the Relationship with Your Parents

As we grow older, the dynamic with our parents often shifts. The balance of care starts to tip, and it becomes our turn to offer support. But nurturing that bond isn't just about physical care; it's about emotional presence. Calling your parents, spending time with them, and showing appreciation for their guidance are simple yet profound acts of love that can strengthen the relationship.

For those who have experienced conflicts or distance with their parents, now is the time to heal those wounds. Life is unpredictable, and waiting too long to repair a parental bond can lead to regret. A simple conversation, an apology, or even just spending time together can mend what was once broken.

4. Conquering the Game of Love: A Path to Redemption and Growth

The Game of Love is not about perfection, nor is it about never making mistakes. It's about how we recover from those mistakes, how we learn to love better, and how we choose to show up for the people who matter most to us. Romantic love, friendships, and parental bonds are all different sides of the same coin—each teaching us valuable lessons in empathy, trust, sacrifice, and resilience.

To truly conquer this game, consider the following key steps:

1. **Self-Reflection and Accountability:** You can't navigate love successfully if you're not willing to take a deep, honest look at yourself. In each relationship, ask yourself: What role have I played in both the highs and lows? Taking accountability for your actions is the first step toward improving any connection.

2. **Consistent Effort and Communication:** No relationship survives on autopilot. Whether it's your romantic partner, your best friend, or your parent, consistent effort is required. Don't wait for special occasions to show you care; make it a habit to regularly express love and appreciation.

3. **Forgiveness and Letting Go of Grudges:** In every relationship, mistakes will be made. People will hurt you, sometimes unintentionally, and you will hurt others. Learning to forgive, and asking for forgiveness, is one of the most powerful ways to heal and strengthen a relationship. Holding onto grudges only deepens wounds.

4. **Prioritizing Emotional Presence:** Being emotionally present means more than just being physically there. It means listening without judgment, offering support without expectation, and

showing up for someone with your whole heart. In the Game of Love, emotional presence is what builds trust and security.

5. **Owning the Game:** Conquering the Game of Love isn't about never falling down—it's about owning your experiences, learning from your mistakes, and choosing to love better each time. Whether it's romantic, friendship, or parental love, the key is to remain open, vulnerable, and willing to grow.

Ultimately, love is not a game you play to win against others; it's a game you play to win within yourself. Each experience, whether filled with joy or heartbreak, offers you a chance to grow, to heal, and to become a better version of yourself. In doing so, you don't just win the Game of Love—you own it, creating deeper, more meaningful connections with those you hold dear.

Chapter 2

The Game of Emotions Joy, Sadness, Anger and Love

Understanding Emotions as a Player in the Game of Life

In the grand game of life, emotions are the invisible force guiding our every action, reaction, and decision. They shape our interactions, influence our choices, and affect our mental and physical well-being. Yet, emotions are often misunderstood and mismanaged, leading to poor decisions, regret, and even broken relationships. To truly master life, one must first learn to understand and navigate the emotional landscape.

Emotions are the unseen players in the game of life. Whether it's joy, sadness, anger, or love, they hold the power to influence outcomes far beyond what we can control through logic alone. Like any player, emotions can either help or hinder us depending on how well we understand them. Learning to manage and direct your emotions is key to conquering this complex game.

1. The Role of Emotions in Our Lives

Emotions are not just fleeting feelings; they are signals. They tell us when something matters, when we need to pay attention, and when we are aligned or misaligned with our true selves. Emotions are essentially our brain's way of communicating what we value.

When you're in love, for example, your emotions heighten your awareness of the person you care about, making you more attentive, kind, and considerate. On the flip side, emotions like anger or jealousy can cloud your judgment and make you act irrationally, damaging relationships and leading to regret. Understanding the role emotions play helps us to engage more consciously in the game of life.

> *"Emotions are not good or bad, they are data.*
> *They inform us about what is happening within*
> *and around us."*

Recognizing this can shift our perspective. Instead of labelling emotions as "negative" or "positive," we can see them for what they truly are—information. How we choose to respond to that information is what ultimately shapes our experiences.

2. Emotional Triggers and Reactions: Identifying Patterns

One of the key aspects of mastering emotions is identifying emotional triggers and patterns. Each of us has certain experiences, words, or actions that trigger strong emotional reactions, often leading to impulsive or regrettable behaviour. The challenge lies in recognizing these triggers before they lead to unwanted outcomes.

For instance, you may find yourself reacting with frustration when someone questions your abilities at work. This frustration could stem from a deeper fear of inadequacy or failure. By identifying the root cause of your emotional reaction, you gain the ability to manage it more effectively. Recognizing triggers isn't just about avoiding negative reactions; it's about understanding why they exist in the first place.

> *"If you can learn to pause before reacting to your emotions, you can change the course of any interaction, conversation, or relationship."*

This pause is where the magic happens. It's where you gain control over the game. Instead of being swept away by emotions, you become the master of them, using your understanding to guide your actions in a more deliberate way.

3. Emotional Intelligence: The Key to Success

Emotional intelligence (EI) is often considered the most important skill in both personal and professional life. It is the ability to recognize, understand, and manage your emotions, as well as to empathize with others' emotions. In the game of life, EI acts as a superpower, giving you the advantage to navigate complex social dynamics, maintain strong relationships, and handle conflicts gracefully.

Imagine a scenario where a colleague criticizes your work. Without EI, you might react defensively, seeing the criticism as an attack. But with EI, you're able to take a step back and assess the situation with a clear mind. You realize that the criticism is not a personal attack but rather feedback that can help you grow. Responding calmly not only preserves your dignity but also strengthens your relationship with the colleague, showing them you are open to improvement.

> *"People with high emotional intelligence aren't just emotionally aware—they are emotionally strategic."*

By being emotionally strategic, you can handle any challenge life throws at you with grace. Whether it's a heated argument, a personal loss, or an exciting new opportunity, your emotional intelligence gives you the ability to remain composed, thoughtful, and effective.

4. Emotional Regulation: Staying in Control

While emotional intelligence helps you understand your emotions, emotional regulation is the ability to control them. Life will always throw curveballs—stressful situations, disappointments, or moments of frustration—but how you manage your emotions in those moments defines your ability to navigate the game successfully.

Think of emotional regulation like a thermostat for your emotional temperature. When you feel yourself getting too hot (angry, anxious, overwhelmed), you need to cool down by employing techniques like deep breathing, mindfulness, or simply stepping away from the situation. Conversely, when you're feeling down or disconnected, you might need to warm yourself up by engaging in positive activities or seeking support from friends or family.

"Emotional regulation is not about suppressing emotions but about managing them in a way that serves your best interest."

A player who knows how to regulate their emotions can stay calm in the storm. They can maintain focus and clarity, even in high-stress environments, which makes them a force to be reckoned with in any aspect of life.

5. The Balance Between Logic and Emotion

There is often a misconception that emotions are irrational and must be ignored in favour of logic. However, true mastery of life comes from balancing logic with emotion. Emotions provide valuable insights, but logic ensures that we act in ways that align with our long-term goals.

For example, in romantic relationships, emotions like love and attraction are essential, but they should be balanced with logic. Just because you feel a strong emotional connection with someone doesn't mean they are the right partner for you long-term. Similarly, in business, passion and drive can fuel your success, but logical decision-making is what ensures sustainability and growth.

> *"When you learn to integrate both logic and emotion, you make decisions that are not only aligned with your goals but also with your values."*

This balance is crucial in every area of life. Ignoring emotions can lead to burnout, dissatisfaction, and poor relationships. But letting emotions rule unchecked can lead to impulsive decisions and chaos. The key is to recognize when to rely on logic and when to let your emotions guide you.

6. Mastering Emotions in Conflict

Conflict is an inevitable part of life, whether in your personal relationships, workplace, or even with yourself. Learning to manage your emotions during conflict is a crucial aspect of mastering the game of life.

When emotions run high in conflict, it's easy to say things we don't mean, make rash decisions, or escalate the situation. But emotions, when harnessed correctly, can also lead to resolution and deeper understanding.

For example, if you're in a disagreement with a loved one, it's tempting to let your emotions take control and lash out. But by pausing, identifying what emotions you're feeling (hurt, frustration, fear), and expressing them calmly, you open the door for constructive dialogue. Emotional awareness allows both parties to understand each other's perspectives, leading to a resolution that strengthens the relationship rather than damages it.

> *"Conflict is not the end of a relationship—it's the beginning of a deeper understanding if you manage your emotions wisely."*

By mastering your emotions in moments of conflict, you not only preserve your relationships but also build emotional resilience, making you stronger for future challenges.

7. Building Emotional Resilience: The Key to Winning the Game

Life will always present challenges—unexpected losses, setbacks, and disappointments. Emotional resilience is your ability to bounce back from these difficulties, using them as opportunities for growth rather than as reasons to give up.

Resilience doesn't mean you won't feel sadness, fear, or anger in the face of adversity. It means that you have the strength and emotional tools to process those feelings and move forward. Whether it's through journaling, therapy, meditation, or simply talking to a trusted friend, building resilience is about facing your emotions head-on and learning from them.

> *"Emotional resilience isn't about never falling—it's about always getting back up."*

In the game of life, resilience is what separates those who merely survive from those who thrive. Every setback is a lesson, every failure is a stepping stone, and every painful emotion is a teacher guiding you toward a better version of yourself.

8. Conclusion: Owning Your Emotions, Owning the Game

Understanding your emotions is not a sign of weakness; it's a sign of strength. In the game of life, those who master their emotions hold the ultimate power. They are not slaves to their feelings but instead use their emotions as tools for growth, connection, and success.

To own your emotions is to own the game. By practicing self-awareness, emotional regulation, and empathy, you become a player who is not only in control of your own life but also capable of inspiring and positively influencing the lives of others.

The Game of Life is won not by those who never feel but by those who know how to feel deeply, navigate those feelings, and use them to fuel their journey toward personal fulfilment and meaningful relationships. In the end, mastering your emotions means mastering the game itself.

The Power of Emotional Intelligence in the Game of Life

In the grand game of life, the ability to navigate the ups and downs is largely dependent on one's emotional intelligence (EI). While IQ measures cognitive abilities, EI is what allows us to build deep relationships, handle stress, and make thoughtful decisions that align with our values. It's the invisible force behind successful interpersonal dynamics, personal growth, and resilience in the face of adversity. When we speak of "winning" in life, we are not referring to superficial achievements, but rather the deep, meaningful victories that arise from a place of emotional awareness and maturity.

In the context of life being a game, emotional intelligence is your strategy guide. It's the key to unlocking relationships, managing conflict, and ultimately thriving in every facet of life. Whether it's love, friendship, or career, your ability to understand and manage emotions—both yours and others'—determines your success.

1. What is Emotional Intelligence?

Emotional intelligence is the ability to perceive, understand, manage, and regulate emotions. It's about being aware of your emotional state and using that awareness to navigate complex social situations and relationships effectively. But it's not just about you; EI also involves being attuned to others' emotions and responding with empathy and care. The concept, popularized by Daniel Goleman, is broken down into five core components:

Self-awareness: Recognizing and understanding your emotions as they happen.

Self-regulation: The ability to control or redirect disruptive emotions and impulses.

Motivation: Being driven to achieve for the sake of achievement, not just external rewards.

Empathy: Understanding and sharing the feelings of others, which fosters better relationships.

Social skills: Managing relationships to move people in desired directions.

> *"Emotional intelligence is the ability to recognize emotions, reason with emotions, and manage emotions in oneself and others."*

These elements are not just soft skills; they are the building blocks of how you navigate the game of life. They influence every interaction you have, the choices you make, and how resilient you are in the face of challenges.

Self-Awareness: The First Step to Mastery

The first and perhaps most important component of emotional intelligence is self-awareness. You can't control or manage something you don't fully understand. Self-awareness means recognizing your own emotional state, understanding what triggers those emotions, and knowing how they influence your behaviour.

Imagine you're in a heated argument with a loved one. If you're unaware of your emotions, you might lash out in anger, say things you don't mean, or escalate the situation unnecessarily. But if you're emotionally aware, you can recognize the anger rising within you and choose to pause, take a breath, and respond more calmly.

> *"Self-awareness is like holding a mirror to your soul. You see your true self—flaws, strengths, and everything in between."*

This awareness isn't about suppressing emotions or ignoring them; it's about understanding their roots. By doing so, you can make conscious choices instead of reacting impulsively. In the game of life, those who master self-awareness gain the ability to respond wisely, rather than act out of raw emotion.

Self-Regulation: Controlling the Game's Tempo

Self-regulation is the ability to control or redirect disruptive emotions, particularly during stressful situations. It's the difference between reacting impulsively and responding thoughtfully. In the game of life, situations often arise where we're tested—whether it's conflict, rejection, or failure. The ability to regulate your emotional response in these moments is crucial.

Think of a high-stakes moment in your life, perhaps a job interview or a confrontation with a friend. Without self-regulation, nerves or anger could take over, causing you to behave in ways that could jeopardize your goals. However, with strong self-regulation, you maintain composure, think clearly, and make decisions that align with your long-term objectives.

> *"Mastering self-regulation means*
> *you control your emotions;*
> *they don't control you."*

This skill becomes especially important in relationships. In the heat of an argument, for example, emotions like frustration or resentment can flare up. But self-regulation allows you to step back, assess the situation, and choose a more constructive response. This doesn't mean ignoring or bottling up your feelings, but rather acknowledging them and deciding how best to act upon them.

Motivation: The Emotional Drive to Succeed

Motivation in the context of emotional intelligence is not just about external rewards like money or status; it's about an inner drive to grow, improve, and succeed. People with high emotional intelligence are motivated by more than just accolades or recognition—they are driven by personal fulfilment, purpose, and passion.

When you're emotionally intelligent, setbacks or failures don't deter you because your motivation comes from within. You're playing the game of life with a deeper sense of purpose, and that purpose drives you to keep going, even when the odds are against you.

For example, consider a person who is working to repair a broken relationship. If they're only motivated by a desire to win back approval or avoid loneliness, they might not put in the necessary emotional effort. But if they're driven by a genuine desire to improve themselves and the relationship, they'll persevere through tough conversations, reflect on their actions, and remain committed to positive change.

> *"True motivation comes from within,*
> *and it's what fuels you when external*
> *rewards fall short."*

Motivation, in this sense, keeps you playing the game with integrity. It's what pushes you to work on your relationships, to pursue your dreams, and to grow as a person.

Empathy: The Secret Weapon in the Game

Empathy is the ability to understand and share the feelings of others. In the game of life, empathy is your secret weapon for building and maintaining relationships. When you're able to step into someone else's shoes and see the world from their perspective, you create deeper connections, resolve conflicts more effectively, and foster trust.

Empathy doesn't mean agreeing with everyone or sacrificing your own needs. Rather, it's about being able to understand where someone else is coming from, even if their perspective differs from your own. In romantic relationships, empathy is what allows you to understand your partner's feelings during a disagreement. In friendships, it's what helps you offer support when your friend is going through a tough time.

For example, if a friend lashes out at you unexpectedly, empathy allows you to recognize that their anger might stem from something deeper—stress at work, personal insecurities, or unresolved trauma. By responding with empathy rather than defensiveness, you can address the root cause of the issue, rather than just the surface-level conflict.

> *"Empathy is the bridge that connects us to others, allowing us to build trust, resolve conflicts, and deepen relationships."*

In the game of life, empathy is often what sets successful people apart. It allows you to navigate complex social situations with grace, build meaningful relationships, and create environments of mutual understanding.

Social Skills: Winning with People

Social skills are the final, outward manifestation of emotional intelligence. While self-awareness, self-regulation, motivation, and empathy are internal processes, social skills are how you put emotional intelligence into action in your interactions with others. This includes communication, conflict resolution, collaboration, and leadership.

People with strong social skills know how to navigate complex social dynamics, whether in a personal relationship or a professional setting. They are adept at building rapport, listening actively, and communicating clearly. They understand the importance of body language, tone, and timing in conveying messages.

In the game of life, social skills are your ability to "win with people." It's not about manipulation or using others to get ahead; it's about creating positive interactions that benefit everyone involved. Whether you're negotiating a business deal, resolving a dispute with a friend, or simply trying to make someone feel heard, social skills help you succeed.

> *"Success in life is not just about what you know—it's about how well you connect with others."*

This aspect of emotional intelligence is particularly important in leadership. Great leaders are not just knowledgeable or skilled; they are emotionally intelligent. They know how to inspire, motivate, and lead others by connecting on a human level. In friendships and romantic relationships, social skills allow you to maintain harmony, address issues before they escalate, and create environments where both parties feel valued and understood.

2. How to Cultivate Emotional Intelligence

Like any skill, emotional intelligence can be developed and strengthened with practice. Here are a few strategies to cultivate EI:

Practice mindfulness: Mindfulness helps you stay present, aware of your emotions, and in control of your reactions. Regular mindfulness practice can increase self-awareness and improve emotional regulation.

Reflect on your emotional experiences: Journaling or simply reflecting on your emotional experiences can help you understand your emotional triggers, patterns, and responses.

Develop active listening skills: To build empathy and social skills, practice active listening. This means fully engaging with the person speaking, offering validation, and responding thoughtfully.

Seek feedback: Ask trusted friends or colleagues for feedback on your emotional intelligence. This can provide valuable insights into how you're perceived and where you can improve.

Work on conflict resolution: Practice addressing conflicts calmly and constructively. Focus on understanding the other person's perspective and finding mutually beneficial solutions.

"Emotional intelligence isn't something you're born with—it's something you can develop through conscious effort and practice."

3. Conclusion: Emotional Intelligence as the Ultimate Game Strategy

In the game of life, emotional intelligence is the ultimate strategy for success. It's not just about winning in the traditional sense, but about navigating life's complexities with grace, wisdom, and emotional depth. By cultivating emotional intelligence, you can improve your relationships, make better decisions, and create a life that's not only successful but also meaningful.

Whether it's self-awareness, self-regulation, motivation, empathy, or social skills, each aspect of emotional intelligence equips you with the tools to play the game of life at a higher level. By mastering your emotions, understanding others, and navigating social dynamics skilfully, you position yourself for lasting success—both in your personal relationships and in the broader game of life.

Handling Negative Emotions: Anger, Sadness, and Fear

Negative emotions are an inevitable part of life. No matter how hard we try, we can't avoid feeling angry, sad, or afraid at some point in our lives. These emotions are not just reactions to the difficulties we face; they are integral parts of our emotional spectrum, guiding us through challenges, signalling when something is wrong, and helping us grow. In the game of life, handling negative emotions can be one of the most challenging but rewarding tasks. It's easy to get consumed by them, to allow anger to dictate your actions, sadness to paralyze you, or fear to stop you from moving forward. However, the true mastery of life—owning it rather than just participating in it—comes from learning to manage and channel these emotions in ways that foster growth rather than destruction.

In this chapter, we'll dive into the emotional depths of anger, sadness, and fear, exploring their origins, impacts, and the strategies to manage them effectively. We will also look at how emotional intelligence plays a key role in handling these emotions, and how mastering them can transform not only our relationships but also our personal well-being.

1. Anger: The Fire That Burns Within

Anger is one of the most powerful and, often, the most destructive emotions. It can rise in a flash, like a wildfire, igniting everything in its path, leaving relationships and situations in ruins. But anger, when understood and managed, can also be a force for good—a motivator for change, a signal that something needs to be addressed, a fire that can fuel us to stand up for ourselves or others.

The Origins of Anger

At its core, anger is a response to perceived injustice, threat, or frustration. It stems from feeling that something is wrong—whether it's someone crossing your boundaries, being disrespected, or facing a situation where you feel powerless. Anger is a protective emotion, a way for your mind and body to defend against external or internal threats.

However, anger is often misunderstood. Many people see it as a "bad" emotion, something to suppress or avoid. In reality, anger is neither good nor bad; it's simply an emotional response that, when channelled correctly, can be beneficial.

For instance, if someone repeatedly disrespects your boundaries, anger can be the emotional fuel that drives you to stand up for yourself. If there's an injustice in society, anger can spark movements for social change. The key lies in how we manage anger and whether we let it control us or we control it.

The Destructive Power of Uncontrolled Anger

When left unchecked, anger can destroy everything in its path. In relationships, uncontrolled anger leads to hurtful words, actions we later regret, and even violence. It can push away loved ones, damage trust, and leave deep emotional scars. In the heat of anger, people often say and do things that cause irreparable harm—whether it's lashing out at a partner, yelling at a child, or physically harming someone.

But beyond the external damage, anger can also corrode us from the inside. Chronic anger leads to health issues, including high blood pressure, heart problems, and anxiety. It can distort our thinking, making us see the world through a lens of hostility and resentment, pushing us further into isolation and bitterness.

> *"Anger is like a fire. If you let it consume you,*
> *it will burn everything to the ground.*
> *But if you learn to control it, you can use its*
> *heat to forge something stronger."*

Channelling Anger for Positive Change

The goal isn't to eliminate anger but to learn how to channel it. One of the most effective ways to manage anger is to develop emotional intelligence—specifically, self-awareness and self-regulation. When you feel anger rising, take a moment to acknowledge it without acting on it immediately. Ask yourself: Why am I feeling this way? What triggered this emotion? Is my anger justified, or am I reacting impulsively?

Once you understand the root of your anger, you can choose how to respond. Instead of lashing out, communicate your feelings assertively. For example, instead of yelling at your partner for not helping around the house, say, "I feel overwhelmed and unappreciated when I have to handle everything on my own. Can we work together to share the responsibilities?" This approach expresses your emotions without causing harm, fostering understanding instead of conflict.

Physical activity, mindfulness practices, and deep breathing are also effective ways to dissipate the intense energy that comes with anger. By calming your body and mind, you give yourself the space to think clearly and respond thoughtfully.

Turning Anger into a Force for Good

Anger can also be a powerful motivator for positive change. Think of the great social movements in history—civil rights, women's rights, LGBTQ+ rights—all fuelled by collective anger at injustice. On a personal level, anger can motivate you to take control of your life, whether it's standing up to a toxic boss, leaving an abusive relationship, or setting boundaries with people who've taken advantage of your kindness.

The key to harnessing anger for good is to ensure that it's aligned with your values and directed toward constructive actions. Instead of letting anger fester and turn into resentment or revenge, use it to fuel change, growth, and healing.

2. Sadness: The Depths of Emotion

Sadness is often seen as the opposite of happiness, but it's so much more than that. It's a deeply introspective emotion, one that pulls us into the depths of our being, forcing us to confront our vulnerabilities, losses, and unmet desires. While sadness is painful, it is also one of the most human emotions—it connects us to our hearts, to our longing for connection, and to the fragility of life.

The Role of Sadness in the Game of Life

Sadness is usually triggered by loss, disappointment, or feelings of helplessness. It could be the loss of a loved one, the end of a relationship, failure in a career, or unmet expectations. In the game of life, we all encounter setbacks and losses, and sadness is the emotional response that follows.

While many people try to avoid sadness at all costs, it plays a crucial role in our emotional landscape. It gives us the space to process grief, to mourn what we've lost, and to reflect on what truly matters. Sadness can be the emotional ground zero from which we rebuild our lives after tragedy or failure.

> *"Sadness is not weakness. It is the soul's way of healing after being wounded."*

The Dangers of Suppressing Sadness

In a world that often values positivity and success, many people feel pressured to hide their sadness, to "keep it together" and move on quickly. However, suppressing sadness can lead to emotional numbness, depression, and even physical health issues.

When you suppress sadness, you also suppress your ability to connect deeply with others. Genuine human connection comes from vulnerability, and sadness is one of the emotions that allows us to be vulnerable. When you share your sadness with a trusted friend or loved one, it opens the door to deeper intimacy and understanding.

On the other hand, if you bottle up your sadness, it festers and can turn into chronic despair or bitterness. It can also manifest in other unhealthy ways, such as addictions, compulsive behaviours, or emotional detachment.

Embracing Sadness as Part of the Healing Process

The key to handling sadness is not to avoid it but to embrace it as part of the healing process. Just as the body needs time to recover from physical injuries, the heart and mind need time to heal from emotional wounds.

One way to embrace sadness is to allow yourself to feel it fully without judgment. Instead of labelling sadness as "bad" or something to get rid of, see it as a natural response to loss or disappointment. By accepting your sadness, you create the emotional space for healing to occur.

Talking about your sadness with a trusted friend, family member, or therapist can also help. Often, just the act of putting your feelings into words can provide relief and clarity. It can also remind you that you're not alone—sadness is a universal human experience, and sharing it can bring you closer to others.

Finding Meaning in Sadness

Sadness, while painful, can also be a pathway to growth and deeper meaning. It forces us to confront the fragility of life, to reflect on what we truly value, and to appreciate the moments of joy and connection we might otherwise take for granted.

For example, the loss of a loved one can be devastating, but it can also remind us of the importance of love and connection in our lives. It can prompt us to cherish the relationships we have, to forgive past wrongs, and to live more fully in the present.

In this way, sadness can be a teacher, guiding us toward a more compassionate, reflective, and meaningful life.

3. Fear: The Shadow That Holds Us Back

Fear is a primal emotion, rooted in our survival instinct. It alerts us to danger and prepares our bodies to respond—whether through fight, flight, or freeze. But in the modern world, fear often goes beyond physical threats. We fear failure, rejection, vulnerability, the unknown, and even success. While fear can be a helpful guide in certain situations, it can also hold us back, preventing us from taking risks, pursuing our dreams, and forming meaningful connections.

Understanding the Nature of Fear

Fear is not inherently bad. In fact, it's essential for survival. It's what keeps us from walking into traffic, touching fire, or jumping off cliffs. But in the game of life, fear often extends beyond physical danger and manifests in more complex ways. We fear being judged, making mistakes, or not living up to expectations. We fear change, even when it's necessary for our growth.

At its core, fear is a response to uncertainty and perceived threat. It tells us, "Something is not safe here." The challenge is that our brains often interpret emotional or social risks as physical threats, triggering the same fear response that would be appropriate if we were in actual danger.

"Fear is a shadow that grows when you turn your back on it. Face it, and it shrinks to reveal the path forward."

The Paralysis of Fear

When fear takes over, it can paralyze us. It can stop us from speaking up, from trying something new, or from making a necessary change in our lives. Fear of failure can keep us stuck in jobs we hate or relationships that no longer serve us. Fear of rejection can prevent us from forming deep, meaningful connections with others.

This paralysis is often rooted in a desire for control. We fear the unknown because we can't control it, and we fear vulnerability because it means opening ourselves up to the possibility of pain. But in trying to avoid these risks, we often miss out on the very things that make life worth living—love, growth, adventure, and fulfillment.

Courage: Moving Forward Despite Fear

The antidote to fear is not the absence of it, but the courage to move forward despite it. Courage doesn't mean you don't feel fear; it means you acknowledge the fear but choose to act anyway. It's the willingness to take risks, to face uncertainty, and to embrace vulnerability.

One of the most powerful ways to develop courage is through self-awareness and emotional intelligence. By understanding your fears—what triggers them, where they come from—you can begin to challenge them. Ask yourself: Is this fear rational? What's the worst that could happen if I face it? Often, just the act of questioning your fear can diminish its power.

Surrounding yourself with supportive, encouraging people can also help you move forward despite fear. When you have a network of friends, family, or mentors who believe in you, it becomes easier to take risks and face challenges.

Fear as a Guide for Growth

Instead of seeing fear as something to avoid, try reframing it as a guide for growth. Fear often points us toward the areas of our lives where we need to grow the most. For example, if you're afraid of public speaking, that's a sign that developing this skill could be an important part of your personal or professional growth. If you're afraid of vulnerability in relationships, it might indicate that deepening your emotional connections is the next step in your personal development.

By facing your fears head-on, you not only conquer them but also open yourself up to new possibilities and experiences. Each time you step out of your comfort zone and face a fear, you expand your sense of what's possible and build resilience for future challenges.

4. Mastering Negative Emotions: The Key to Owning the Game of Life

Anger, sadness, and fear are powerful emotions that, if left unchecked, can lead to destruction and paralysis. But when understood and managed effectively, these emotions become tools for growth, healing, and transformation.

By developing emotional intelligence—particularly self-awareness, self-regulation, and empathy—you can learn to navigate these emotions in a way that not only minimizes their negative impact but also harnesses their power for positive change.

In the game of life, owning your emotions—rather than letting them own you—is key to living a life that's not only successful but also meaningful.

Whether it's self-awareness, self-regulation, motivation, empathy, or social skills, each aspect of emotional intelligence equips you with the tools to play the game of life at a higher level. By mastering your emotions, understanding others, and navigating social dynamics skillfully, you position yourself for lasting success—both in your personal relationships and in the broader game of life.

The Balance Between Logic and Emotion: Mastering the Inner Tug-of-War

In the complex game of life, there is a constant tug-of-war between two powerful forces: logic and emotion. Both are integral to human existence, yet they often appear to pull us in opposite directions. Logic tells us to think rationally, to calculate, to plan, and to make decisions based on facts. Emotion, on the other hand, urges us to feel, to react, to connect with our instincts and desires. Finding a balance between these two forces is one of life's most profound challenges. Without balance, we risk either becoming overly analytical, detached, and cold, or excessively emotional, impulsive, and out of control. But when we can master this balance, we can make sound decisions that honor both our minds and hearts, ultimately owning the game of life.

This chapter explores the intricacies of logic and emotion, how they influence our decision-making, and why it's essential to integrate both into our lives. We'll dive into how emotion and logic interact in different areas—relationships, personal growth, and professional life—examining how to harness their power without letting either dominate in ways that lead to regret or imbalance.

1. The Nature of Logic and Emotion

Logic is defined by reason and rationality. It's the analytical part of our brain that evaluates situations, calculates risks, and draws conclusions based on evidence. Logic gives us structure. It's what allows us to strategize, create plans, and solve problems systematically. Logic is indispensable when it comes to making decisions that require careful thought, such as managing finances, developing career goals, or navigating complex problems.

On the other hand, **emotion** is deeply connected to our feelings, instincts, and desires. Emotions are the colors of our inner world, giving life to our experiences. They fuel our passions, our motivations, and our connections with others. Emotions guide us toward pleasure and away from pain. They are the driving force behind the connections we form, the love we feel, and the compassion we show. Emotions are crucial for empathy, for understanding others, and for living a life filled with meaning and depth.

But emotions are also volatile. They can be unpredictable and overpowering. When emotions run high, they can cloud our judgment, leading us to make decisions based on impulse rather than reason. Yet, suppressing emotions in favor of cold logic can leave us feeling disconnected from ourselves and those we care about.

The goal is not to choose one over the other but to create a harmonious balance between the two.

2. Emotional Decision-Making: The Heart's Influence

Emotional decision-making is driven by our feelings and instincts. When we make decisions based on emotion, we often react quickly, guided by our internal desires, fears, and needs. Emotions can be incredibly powerful in shaping our choices, especially when it comes to relationships, personal desires, and life changes.

In Love and Relationships

When it comes to love, emotion is often the leading force. Love is, at its core, an emotional experience. We fall in love not because it is logical or makes sense, but because it stirs something deep within us. Love, compassion, and empathy are all emotional responses that shape our bonds with others. Emotional decision-making in relationships allows us to connect deeply, to nurture, to forgive, and to build trust.

However, unchecked emotional responses in relationships can also lead to impulsive actions, jealousy, and misunderstandings. For example, an emotionally driven decision to confront a partner in a moment of anger or jealousy might damage trust and cause unnecessary conflict. Conversely, allowing emotions like empathy and understanding to guide responses in conflict can strengthen the relationship.

In Career and Personal Growth

Emotion also plays a significant role in personal growth and career choices. People often feel called to certain professions based on passion—an emotional response to something that deeply moves or excites them. But emotions like fear can hold someone back from taking a leap of faith or making significant changes in their lives. An overwhelming sense of security might drive someone to stay in a job they hate rather than pursue a more fulfilling career.

It's clear that emotion shapes much of how we live and experience life. It fuels our passions and dreams, but without the guiding hand of logic, it can also trap us in fear or cause us to make impulsive decisions we may regret later.

"Emotions are the language of the heart,
and logic is the voice of the mind. To live fully,
we must listen to both."

3. Logical Decision-Making: The Mind's Control

On the flip side, logical decision-making is rooted in analysis, evidence, and careful consideration of consequences. It's the side of us that calculates risks, weighs pros and cons, and seeks the most rational solution to a problem. In many cases, logical thinking can prevent us from making rash decisions based on fleeting emotions.

In Relationships

In relationships, logic helps us to step back and analyse situations objectively. When emotions run high—during arguments or moments of misunderstanding—logic allows us to reflect before reacting. It helps prevent unnecessary conflicts, providing clarity and perspective. For example, after a heated argument, logic tells us to give space, cool down, and think through what happened before continuing the conversation.

Yet, relying too much on logic in relationships can cause us to lose touch with the emotional needs of our partners. Overanalysing everything can take the spontaneity and joy out of a relationship. Love and connection are not purely logical; they require emotional expression, vulnerability, and empathy.

In Personal and Professional Life

In professional settings, logic is crucial for making sound business decisions. It helps in setting long-term goals, analysing risks, and creating strategies. Without logical thinking, it would be impossible to navigate complex career paths, investments, or personal growth plans.

However, an overly logical approach can also stifle creativity and innovation. Logic might convince you to stick with what's safe, rather than take a bold risk that could lead to greater personal or professional fulfilment.

When we overly rely on logic, we can become disconnected from our emotional experiences and the things that truly matter to us on a personal level. A career that is based solely on rational decisions may bring financial success but could leave one feeling unfulfilled if it lacks passion or purpose.

*"Logic may get you where you need to go,
but it is emotion that tells you where
you truly belong."*

4. The Struggle for Balance: Why It's Difficult

Finding the right balance between logic and emotion is not easy. Humans are inherently emotional creatures, and often, our emotions feel more immediate and pressing than our logical thoughts. When faced with decisions, especially those that evoke strong feelings—such as romantic relationships, family conflicts, or career dilemmas—our first instinct is often to react emotionally.

Yet, life demands that we also think critically and plan ahead. Without logic, we would be overwhelmed by our emotions, unable to make thoughtful choices that align with our long-term goals. On the other hand, if we suppress our emotions in favour of cold, rational thinking, we lose touch with the richness of our human experience.

So why is balance so difficult to achieve? Because it requires awareness, mindfulness, and self-regulation. It's easy to let our emotions take over, especially in moments of stress, anger, or fear. Similarly, it's tempting to retreat into logic when emotions feel too intense or overwhelming. But living a fulfilled life means learning to embrace both logic and emotion and knowing when to lean into each.

5. Finding the Balance: Strategies for Success

1. Develop Emotional Intelligence

Emotional intelligence (EI) is the ability to recognize, understand, and manage your emotions and the emotions of others. High EI allows you to be aware of your emotional state and how it influences your thinking and actions. By developing emotional intelligence, you can become more skilled at recognizing when emotions are driving your decisions and when it's time to step back and apply logic.

2. Practice Mindfulness

Mindfulness is the practice of being present in the moment without judgment. By practicing mindfulness, you can become more aware of your thoughts and emotions, allowing you to pause before reacting impulsively. Mindfulness helps you observe your emotional responses without getting caught up in them, giving you the space to make more balanced decisions.

3. Create a Decision-Making Process

When faced with important decisions, it can be helpful to create a structured decision-making process that takes both logic and emotion into account. Start by identifying the facts and logical considerations— what are the pros and cons? What are the potential risks? Then, take a moment to reflect on how you feel about the decision. What are your gut instincts telling you? How will this decision affect your emotional well-being? By consciously including both logic and emotion in the process, you can make more balanced choices.

4. Take Time to Reflect

One of the best ways to find balance is to take time before making decisions, especially when strong emotions are involved. Whether it's a heated argument with a loved one or a major life decision, giving yourself space to cool down and reflect can prevent emotional impulsivity. During this time, write down your thoughts and feelings to gain clarity. Once you've had a chance to process your emotions, revisit the situation with a clearer, more balanced perspective.

5. Embrace Vulnerability and Compassion

In relationships, finding the balance between logic and emotion often requires vulnerability and compassion. Being logical doesn't mean you suppress your feelings; it means you approach situations with understanding and empathy while keeping your emotions in check. Being open about your feelings, while also considering your partner's perspective, creates a foundation for healthy communication and emotional growth.

6. Embracing the Duality of Human Nature

The beauty of life lies in the duality of human nature. We are creatures of both logic and emotion, and to fully experience life, we must honour both. Emotions give life meaning—they drive us toward connection, love, and fulfilment. Logic gives life structure—it helps us navigate challenges, set goals, and create strategies for success. Together, they form a powerful combination that, when balanced, allows us to live with intention and purpose.

In the end, life is a game of choices, and each decision we make is influenced by both our hearts and our minds. By learning to balance logic and emotion, we not only make wiser decisions but also experience the fullness of life's richness.

Chapter 3

The Game of Seduction

The Art of Attraction

Seduction is often misunderstood. It's not merely about physical allure, but an intricate dance of energy, confidence, and connection. The art of attraction is about how you carry yourself, how you make someone feel, and the subtle ways you create desire. In the game of seduction, you are not chasing someone; instead, you are drawing them toward you through your presence, your words, and the unspoken signals you send. The beauty of seduction lies in its elegance and patience—moving slowly and deliberately to create a genuine connection.

In this chapter, we will explore how to master the art of attraction, diving deep into the psychological and emotional aspects of what makes one person irresistible to another. Seduction is a game, and like any game, it requires skill, practice, and an understanding of the rules. It is a slow, tantalizing dance that, when performed well, becomes both powerful and rewarding.

1. Confidence: The Foundation of Seduction

Confidence is the first and most important element of seduction. It's not just about looking good or being charming, but truly believing in your own worth. People are drawn to those who are comfortable in their own skin—those who project an aura of self-assuredness without arrogance.

The Energy of Confidence: Confidence radiates an energy that is hard to resist. When you walk into a room, your posture, your eye contact, and the way you engage with others silently communicate your level of confidence. It's not about being the loudest person in the room but about having a quiet self-assurance that naturally attracts others.

Self-Acceptance: True confidence comes from self-acceptance. When you embrace who you are, flaws and all, you give off a sense of security and strength that others find compelling. This doesn't mean you don't work on improving yourself, but that you accept and love who you are in the present moment.

The Power of Authenticity: Confidence doesn't mean pretending to be someone you're not. In fact, trying to be something you're not is a quick way to kill attraction. Authenticity is key. People are drawn to those who are real and genuine. When you are authentic, you allow others to feel safe around you, which builds deeper connections.

"Confidence is silent. Insecurities are loud."

2. Body Language: The Unspoken Dance

In seduction, words are often secondary to what your body is saying. Body language can communicate desire, interest, and vulnerability without a single word being spoken. Learning how to use your body effectively in the art of attraction is crucial.

The Power of Eye Contact: One of the most potent tools in seduction is eye contact. Holding someone's gaze for just a moment longer than usual creates a sense of intimacy and intrigue. It's a way to connect on a deeper, almost primal level. But remember, eye contact should be natural, not forced. Too much intensity too soon can come off as creepy or overbearing.

Touch and Proximity: Touch, when done right, can be electric. A light touch on the arm, a casual brush of the hand—these small gestures can create a strong physical connection. However, timing and context are key. You must read the situation carefully to determine when touch is appropriate and how much is too much. Personal space and proximity also play a role. Leaning in slightly when speaking to someone, without invading their space, creates a sense of closeness.

Mirroring: One effective yet subtle body language technique is mirroring. This means subtly copying the gestures and posture of the person you are attracted to. Mirroring creates a subconscious bond and makes the other person feel more comfortable around you. However, it should be natural and not forced.

> *"What you say can attract someone for a moment, but how you move will captivate them forever."*

3. The Dance of Words: Communication in Seduction

While body language is powerful, the way you communicate with words also plays a critical role in attraction. Seductive communication isn't about what you say, but how you say it. The tone of your voice, the rhythm of your speech, and the topics you choose can either draw someone in or push them away.

Slow and Deliberate Speech: In the art of seduction, slow and deliberate speech is far more effective than rapid-fire conversation. Taking your time when speaking allows you to be more thoughtful and composed. It also makes the listener hang on to your every word, creating an atmosphere of suspense and intrigue.

The Power of Suggestion: Seduction often involves hinting at deeper feelings or desires without explicitly stating them. The power of suggestion allows the other person to fill in the blanks, which makes them more engaged in the interaction. Subtle compliments, teasing, or playful banter can create a dynamic where both parties feel excited and curious.

Listening More Than Speaking: A great seducer listens more than they speak. When you show genuine interest in someone, it makes them feel valued and important. Listening allows you to understand what the other person needs and desires, giving you the opportunity to respond in a way that deepens the connection. People are attracted to those who make them feel heard and understood.

> *"Seduction is not about what you say,*
> *but how deeply you listen."*

4. Creating Emotional Connection: The Heart of Seduction

Attraction may begin with physical or verbal cues, but seduction truly happens on an emotional level. If you want to attract someone in a lasting way, you must connect with their emotions. This goes beyond flirting or surface-level charm—this is about creating a bond that feels genuine and meaningful.

Vulnerability: One of the most powerful ways to create emotional attraction is by allowing yourself to be vulnerable. Sharing your fears, dreams, and insecurities in a way that is honest and open invites the other person to do the same. Vulnerability breeds intimacy, and when done at the right time, it can turn an attraction into a deeper emotional bond.

Empathy and Understanding: Showing empathy—genuinely caring about the other person's feelings, experiences, and emotions—is key to building emotional attraction. When you demonstrate that you understand them on a deep level, it creates trust and makes them feel safe with you. This emotional safety is crucial for deeper seduction.

Shared Experiences: Seduction is more than just physical or verbal cues; it's about shared experiences that bond two people together. Whether it's sharing a moment of laughter, a vulnerable conversation, or even a mutual interest, these moments create a sense of "we" that strengthens the emotional connection.

"Emotional seduction is the difference between someone who holds your attention for a moment and someone who captivates your heart."

5. Mystery and Intrigue: Keeping the Flame Alive

Seduction thrives on mystery. The moment everything is laid bare, the intrigue begins to fade. A key element of attraction is creating a sense of curiosity—leaving something unsaid, something to discover later.

Being Unpredictable: One of the easiest ways to maintain mystery is by being unpredictable. Don't be too available or too obvious in your intentions. Keep a little distance now and then, allowing the other person to wonder what you're thinking or feeling. This uncertainty fuels attraction.

Leaving Them Wanting More: Seduction is about pacing. Don't rush to reveal everything about yourself or the relationship. Leave room for curiosity. Ending a conversation or interaction on a high note, leaving the other person wanting more, can keep the attraction alive for longer. Let them think about you even after you've left the room.

"In the game of seduction, the greatest power
lies in what remains a mystery."

6. Patience and Timing: The Gentle Push and Pull

Seduction is a game of patience. It's about knowing when to move forward and when to pull back. Rushing into things too quickly can kill the tension, while waiting too long can make the moment pass. Timing is everything.

The Art of Waiting: Patience is crucial in seduction. Knowing when to take your time, when to hold back, and when to advance is key. Don't be afraid of the slow build-up. Attraction grows in the anticipation of what's to come.

Reading the Signals: Effective seduction means being attuned to the other person's signals. If they're pulling back, don't push harder—give them space. If they're leaning in, move forward. Understanding their rhythm and adapting to it ensures that the seduction is mutual and enjoyable for both parties.

> *"Seduction is like a dance—each step should be measured, intentional, and in tune with your partner."*

7. The Fine Line Between Seduction and Manipulation

Seduction, when executed with grace and authenticity, is a dance of mutual attraction, not a game of control. Yet, it's crucial to recognize the fine line between seduction and manipulation. The essence of seduction is rooted in desire, respect, and emotional connection. When we cross that line into manipulation, we lose the beauty and depth of what true seduction can create.

Respecting Boundaries: In the delicate art of seduction, boundaries are sacred. Attraction may be strong, but there is an elegance in knowing how far to go, when to pause, and when to let desire build naturally. True seduction isn't about pushing; it's about leading with subtlety, knowing that respect fuels the passion you seek. Every glance, every word, and every touch should be a step toward deepening the connection, not a forceful act that disregards the other person's comfort or autonomy. Consent is the ultimate aphrodisiac, for it ensures that what is shared is mutual and authentic.

Genuine Intentions: Seduction at its finest stems from a place of sincerity. When your intentions are pure, the connection you create becomes more meaningful and magnetic. It's not about immediate gratification or conquest—it's about crafting an experience that lingers in the mind and heart. When seduction is driven by the genuine desire to form a real bond, it transcends the physical and becomes something timeless. The allure you create will leave a lasting impression, one that cannot be undone by fleeting moments of manipulation.

To seduce without regard for the other person's feelings or boundaries isn't seduction at all—it's manipulation. And manipulation tarnishes the beauty of connection, turning what could have been an unforgettable moment into something hollow and regrettable.

> *"Seduction without respect is merely manipulation; true allure lies in valuing the one you wish to captivate."*

When you value the person you're drawing in, your seduction becomes a powerful and captivating experience—one that ignites passion, but also trust and mutual desire. This is where true seduction shines, balanced delicately between the thrill of attraction and the reverence of respect.

8. Conclusion: Mastering the Art of Attraction

The art of attraction is a skill that anyone can learn and refine with time. It goes far beyond mere physical appearance or charm; it's rooted in confidence, authenticity, emotional depth, and the right timing. When you understand the nuances of attraction, you can use them to naturally enhance your ability to draw others in. But remember, these techniques must always be approached with sincerity.

Attraction and seduction aren't about control or manipulation. True seduction is the creation of a shared experience of desire, connection, and intimacy. It's about sparking something mutual, where both people feel drawn to one another. By practicing self-awareness, emotional intelligence, and genuine interest in others, you become not only more attractive but also more captivating on a deeper level.

Whether you aim to build a meaningful romantic relationship or simply wish to improve how you connect with people in everyday life, these principles can guide you toward mastering the art of seduction. When applied with honesty and respect, your presence will naturally create a sense of allure.

> *"Seduction is not about possessing someone;*
> *it's about crafting a space where desire and*
> *connection flourish naturally."*

True attraction is about creating an atmosphere that invites connection, allowing both people to feel desired and understood.

Building Confidence and Charisma

Confidence is the pulse of seduction, the magnetic force that draws others to you effortlessly. It's not about being the loudest in the room or always knowing what to say—it's about carrying yourself with a sense of inner power that captivates without words. The moment you walk in with poise, like you belong, others notice. Charisma, the subtle magic of attraction, is born from this very confidence.

Imagine this: You walk into a room, not demanding attention, but commanding it. Your presence is undeniable. Every move you make is intentional, every word is laced with purpose. You radiate an aura that others can't help but be drawn to. That's the power of confidence combined with charisma—a seduction that doesn't chase, but beckons.

But let's strip away the idea that confidence is about perfection. Confidence is about embracing imperfections, knowing that your quirks and flaws are what make you irresistibly real. Seduction starts when you embrace who you are and exude an unapologetic authenticity that becomes the core of your allure.

1. The Dance of Self-Assurance

Confidence is the foundation of seduction. It's not about being the loudest or most noticeable person in the room but rather about having an undeniable presence. Real confidence whispers—it doesn't shout. It's conveyed through subtle cues like standing tall, maintaining eye contact, and moving with a purpose that tells the world you know your worth. Confidence isn't about perfection; it's about embracing your flaws and quirks. These imperfections make you human and, in turn, relatable.

When you exude confidence, others are naturally drawn to you. They can sense your self-assuredness, and it makes them curious. Confidence is magnetic. It tells people, "I'm comfortable with who I am," and that's incredibly seductive. There's no need for bravado or arrogance—just a quiet certainty in yourself.

Seduction isn't about overpowering someone with your presence. It's about inviting them into your world through the sheer force of your self-belief. You don't need to be perfect to be confident. In fact, showing vulnerability, while still maintaining your inner strength, can be one of the most seductive traits of all. True self-assurance makes you irresistible because people are naturally drawn to those who know their worth without needing validation from others.

"Confidence is the silent pulse of seduction—it speaks volumes without saying a word, creating an irresistible allure."

2. Charisma: The Invisible Dance of Connection

Charisma is the art of connection. It's about making others feel like they are the only person in the room, drawing them in with your full attention. Charisma isn't about being the center of attention—it's about making others feel like they are. When you engage someone with genuine interest, you create a bond that is far more powerful than mere attraction. Charisma flows from emotional intelligence, the ability to understand and respond to others' feelings and emotions.

Charismatic people are magnetic because they make others feel seen and heard. Eye contact, a well-timed smile, and genuine engagement with someone's words can turn an ordinary conversation into a memorable experience. Charisma is about leaving a lasting impression. It's not about dominating a conversation but about participating in a way that makes others feel valued.

A charismatic person doesn't just talk; they listen, they react, and they make the person they're speaking to feel important. This is incredibly seductive because, in a world where everyone is vying for attention, to feel truly seen by someone is rare. If you want to be irresistible, focus less on trying to impress others and more on making them feel impressive in your presence.

"Charisma isn't loud; it's the quiet confidence that makes people want to be around you, leaving a lasting imprint long after you've left the room."

3. Mastering Body Language: The Silent Seduction

Body language is a powerful tool in the art of seduction. Long before words are spoken, your body communicates volumes. The way you move, the way you hold yourself, and even the subtleties of your expressions can either draw people in or push them away. Seduction, when done through body language, is about subtlety. It's not the overt gestures but the small, almost imperceptible ones that create tension and attraction.

Maintain eye contact, but don't stare. Let your gaze linger just long enough to suggest interest. Your posture should exude confidence—stand tall, shoulders back, relaxed but purposeful. A simple touch, when done correctly, can be electric. A hand on the arm during a conversation, or a light brush of your fingers as you pass someone, can ignite chemistry without words.

Body language is about teasing—about building anticipation. The goal is to leave someone wondering if that look meant more, if that touch was accidental or intentional. The mystery is what makes it seductive. It's about what isn't said, what isn't done—creating an atmosphere of unspoken desire that hangs in the air. Mastering body language is key to becoming a more seductive presence because it speaks directly to the subconscious, where attraction begins.

"Seduction begins long before words are spoken—it's in the way you move, the way your eyes linger, and the touch that leaves someone wanting more."

4. The Allure of Authenticity: Letting Your True Self Shine

Authenticity is the cornerstone of real seduction. Pretending to be someone you're not may get you short-term attention, but it will never build lasting attraction. People are drawn to those who are unapologetically themselves. When you're genuine, you radiate confidence and ease, which is irresistibly attractive. Authenticity allows others to see you as you are, imperfections and all, and it's those imperfections that make you relatable and human.

Being authentic doesn't mean oversharing or being brutally honest to the point of discomfort. It means being true to yourself—speaking from the heart, acting with integrity, and showing vulnerability when the time is right. Authenticity creates trust, and trust is one of the most seductive qualities you can possess.

When you are genuine, you don't need to try so hard to impress others. People are naturally drawn to your energy because it feels real. Inauthenticity, on the other hand, creates a barrier that keeps people at a distance. If you want to be truly seductive, let go of the desire to be perfect or to fit into someone else's mold. Embrace who you are, and others will be irresistibly drawn to your authenticity.

"Authenticity is the most seductive quality of all—when you are truly yourself, people can't help but be drawn to your unique energy."

5. Timing: The Art of Waiting

Seduction is a game of patience. It's not about rushing in or overwhelming someone with attention. True seduction is about timing—knowing when to lean in and when to pull back. It's about creating a sense of anticipation, of leaving someone wanting more. Patience allows desire to build naturally. In the rush to seduce, many people overlook the power of waiting.

Don't rush the conversation, don't force the connection. Let it build organically. The space between actions is where the tension lies. Give someone time to miss you, to wonder about you. In the world of seduction, less is often more. When you master the art of timing, you create an irresistible pull that keeps others coming back.

Waiting also builds intrigue. People are drawn to mystery, to the unknown. When you give everything too quickly, there's nothing left to discover. Seduction is about the slow reveal, about letting your layers be uncovered gradually. This keeps the other person engaged and curious, which is the key to long-lasting attraction.

"Seduction is about patience—letting desire build slowly, creating anticipation, and allowing the tension to rise with perfect timing."

6. Energy: The Magnetic Pull of Seduction

Your energy is the unseen force that draws people to you. It's the vibe you give off before you even speak, the way your presence can shift the atmosphere in a room. Seduction is less about what you say and more about the energy you exude. Are you open, warm, and inviting? Or are you closed off and defensive? People respond to the energy you project, often without even realizing it.

Positive, confident energy is magnetic. When you're comfortable in your own skin, it shows. You don't have to try to seduce anyone—people will naturally be drawn to your presence. Conversely, negative or insecure energy repels. If you're constantly doubting yourself or worried about how others perceive you, that energy creates a barrier.

Cultivating seductive energy is about being mindful of how you carry yourself and what you project to others. It's about being open to connection, but not desperate for it. It's about creating a warm, inviting atmosphere around you that makes people want to get closer, to learn more about you, and to be part of your world.

"Seduction is about the energy you bring into the room—it's the magnetic force that draws people in, leaving them wanting more of you."

Respecting Boundaries in Seduction

Seduction is an intoxicating dance of desire, where every glance, touch, and whispered word is a step closer to deeper connection. But this dance has rules, and none are more important than respecting the boundaries of the one you wish to allure. True seduction isn't about reckless abandon or taking what isn't freely given—it's about creating a space of mutual yearning, where each person is invited into the other's world, willingly and openly.

When you respect boundaries, you allow seduction to be pure, raw, and irresistible. Boundaries are not restrictions; they are the very canvas upon which the most captivating seduction is painted. Each step toward the other person's desires, each acknowledgment of their comfort, amplifies the longing. Respect doesn't hinder passion; it heightens it, ensuring that when the moment comes, it is not only consensual but intensely fulfilling.

1. The Sensual Power of Boundaries

Boundaries are not barriers; they are the edges of a tantalizing mystery waiting to be unravelled. Think of them as the veil between attraction and intimacy, a delicate threshold that, when approached with sensitivity, turns mere interest into burning desire. Knowing where the other person's boundaries lie, and respecting them, draws out the anticipation. Seduction thrives in that space of "almost," where the pull of attraction becomes unbearable because it is not rushed but savoured.

Imagine the electricity of a moment where a gaze lingers just long enough, but not too long. A touch hovers, close but not quite there, making the skin tingle with the promise of what might come. When you honor someone's boundaries, you show them that you are in tune with their rhythm, waiting for the right moment when both of you are perfectly aligned in your desire.

Respecting boundaries doesn't diminish the heat of seduction—it intensifies it. It builds tension, the kind that leaves you breathless, aching for more, but knowing that the timing must be just right. Boundaries are not the end; they are the beginning of deeper intimacy, a place where trust and desire merge into something even more seductive.

> *"Boundaries are not walls, they are the lines that allow desire to grow stronger, deeper, and more irresistible."*

2. The Dance of Attraction: Reading the Unspoken Cues

In the seductive interplay between two people, much of what happens is unspoken. The true art of seduction lies in understanding these silent signals, knowing when to step forward and when to pull back. Attraction is a dance of energy, and every movement, every breath, and every glance is a part of that rhythm. The key to seduction is learning how to read the other person's tempo, feeling out their boundaries with the grace of a skilled dancer.

The flicker of their eyes, the way their body turns toward or away from you, the subtle shift in their tone—all of these are cues that guide the seduction forward. When someone is comfortable, their body will lean into yours, their laughter will flow freely, and their gaze will linger a little longer. But when their body stiffens, or their voice tightens, they are signalling a boundary. Respecting that moment shows them that you are attentive, aware, and most importantly, considerate.

The seductive power of reading these cues lies in your ability to respond, not with force or pressure, but with elegance. You let the other person know that you see them, you understand their limits, and you are willing to wait for them to invite you closer. This creates an atmosphere of mutual attraction where boundaries are not limits but gateways to something even more thrilling.

"Seduction is about feeling the other person's rhythm, moving in sync, and knowing exactly when to lean in and when to hold back."

3. The Sweet Sensation of Consent: A Shared Seduction

Seduction without consent is like a dance without music—it's empty and forced. True seduction happens when both partners are fully engaged in the moment, willingly and enthusiastically. The power of consent lies in the mutual desire that it creates. When both people want each other, when both are drawn into the game with equal passion, the energy becomes electric.

Asking for consent isn't a cold, clinical act; it's seductive in itself. It shows that you care enough about the other person to want them to feel good about what's happening. A soft whisper of "Is this okay?" or "Do you want me to continue?" can be as seductive as the act itself because it deepens the connection. Consent, given freely and eagerly, becomes a source of even greater pleasure.

There's nothing sexier than knowing that the other person is as caught up in the moment as you are, that they want you just as much as you want them. Consent ensures that the seduction is not one-sided, but a mutual exchange of desire. The magic happens when both people are on the same page, their energies combining to create something unforgettable.

> *"Seduction is the dance of two souls entwined in mutual desire, where consent is the music that guides their steps."*

4. Avoiding Manipulation: Seduction Rooted in Integrity

Seduction can be powerful, but it loses its allure when it slips into manipulation. Manipulation is the enemy of true seduction because it tries to force attraction, rather than allowing it to grow naturally. Seduction is not about tricking someone into wanting you—it's about creating an atmosphere where they choose to be with you of their own free will.

When seduction is rooted in authenticity, it becomes magnetic. People are drawn to sincerity and confidence, not games or deceit. If your intentions are pure, if you are seeking to connect rather than control, the seduction will unfold effortlessly. But if you manipulate—whether through guilt, flattery, or pressure—you will undermine the very attraction you are trying to create.

The best seducers understand that real connection cannot be forced. They know that by being honest, by showing respect, and by allowing the other person the freedom to choose, they create a seduction that is far more powerful and lasting than any manipulative tactic could ever be.

"True seduction is built on respect and honesty; manipulation only destroys the connection you're trying to create."

5. The Trust Factor: Strengthening the Bond Through Respect

Respecting boundaries doesn't just prevent harm—it builds trust. Trust is the glue that holds any relationship together, and in the game of seduction, it's the key to deeper attraction. When someone knows that you will respect their boundaries, they feel safe with you. This safety allows them to relax, to open up, and to let the seduction flow naturally.

Trust is seductive because it makes the other person feel valued. It shows them that you are not just interested in what you can get from them, but that you genuinely care about their well-being. This kind of connection is rare, and it's what turns a fleeting moment of attraction into something lasting and meaningful.

By respecting boundaries, you create an environment where trust can thrive. The more someone trusts you, the more they are willing to let you into their world, to share their deepest desires, and to explore new levels of intimacy. Trust is the foundation of seduction, and without it, no real connection can be made.

"In the dance of seduction, trust is the thread that binds two souls together, making every step more intimate and powerful."

6. Mastering Patience: The Art of Slow Seduction

Seduction is not a race—it's a slow, deliberate journey. One of the most seductive qualities you can possess is patience. Knowing when to pull back, when to give the other person space, and when to let the desire simmer is a skill that sets true seducers apart from the rest. Rushing the process kills the mystery; it snuffs out the slow burn of attraction.

Patience shows that you're confident enough to let the other person come to you in their own time. It's in those moments of waiting, in the silences between words, that attraction grows. The most powerful seductions happen when there's room to breathe, when both people are given the time to fully engage with their emotions and desires.

Being patient doesn't mean being passive—it means being attuned to the other person's pace. It means recognizing when to push forward and when to hold back. When you master patience, you turn seduction into an art form, one that leaves the other person wanting more long after the moment has passed.

"Seduction is the art of waiting, of letting the desire build until it's impossible to resist."

7. Conclusion: The Ethical Seducer

At the heart of true seduction lies respect—respect for boundaries, respect for consent, and respect for the other person's autonomy. Seduction is not about control or manipulation; it's about creating a space where both people can engage in the dance of attraction willingly and with full enthusiasm. When you honour someone's boundaries, you create trust. When you seek their consent, you deepen the connection. And when you approach seduction with integrity, you ensure that the desire you create is genuine, powerful, and lasting.

The game of seduction is about more than just getting what you want—it's about building something meaningful, something that both people can enjoy. It's about turning the fleeting spark of attraction into a roaring fire of mutual desire. And the only way to do that is by respecting the other person, by recognizing their boundaries, and by allowing the seduction to unfold naturally and consensually.

"Seduction is not about taking—it's about inviting the other person into a space where desire can grow, unfettered and unforced."

The Ultimate Art of Seduction: A Journey of Desire, Intimacy, and Unspoken Connection

Seduction is often seen as a fleeting art, an ephemeral encounter of desires and attractions that leave one wanting more. But when explored deeply, seduction transcends physical charm and touches the soul. It's an art form that navigates through unspoken desires, delicate tension, and emotional connection. Mastering the art of seduction is about understanding human emotions and desires, creating experiences so captivating that they become memories etched in time.

True seduction is not a one-time event; it's a journey. It's a subtle dance that begins long before the first physical touch and continues long after. It's about creating an atmosphere, setting a stage where two people can explore each other's depths in a way that's intimate, tantalizing, and unforgettable.

To seduce anyone, you must go beyond the surface. The game isn't about control or manipulation; it's about connection. It's about tapping into primal instincts, but with a touch of grace, intelligence, and authenticity. And remember, the most powerful seductions are not rushed—they simmer slowly, building anticipation and deep emotional ties.

1. The Power of First Impressions: Setting the Stage

Every encounter begins with that first glance, that initial spark of intrigue. Whether it's across a crowded room or a chance meeting in an unexpected place, the first impression is where the game begins. The most seductive people know that the art of attraction starts with body language, the way you carry yourself, and the energy you radiate.

Confidence is the key. Walk with purpose, make eye contact, and smile—not just with your lips, but with your entire presence. Confidence is intoxicating. It tells the world that you know your worth and invites others to get a glimpse of the mystery you embody. There is something undeniably attractive about a person who appears comfortable in their own skin, who moves with ease and assurance.

But confidence should never be confused with arrogance. True seduction is subtle. It's the fleeting touch of your gaze, the way your body subtly moves toward someone without seeming eager. Let your movements be smooth, almost unintentional, as if you're not fully aware of the effect you're having. This creates an aura of mystery, leaving the other person curious, drawn to you without quite understanding why.

In those first moments, less is more. Don't rush into conversation or make a bold move. Let the attraction build in the silence between glances, in the space between where you stand and where they are. Allow tension to grow naturally. The unspoken connection in those first few minutes is what will lay the foundation for deeper seduction later.

2. Captivating Through Conversation: Words as a Tool of Intimacy

Seduction isn't just about what you do; it's about what you say—and how you say it. Words are incredibly powerful. They can create entire worlds in the mind of the person you wish to seduce. When used skilfully, words can be the most intimate tool in your arsenal.

Speak in a **low, deliberate tone**. Let your words roll off your tongue slowly, creating a rhythm that pulls the other person in. When you speak slowly, it forces them to hang on to every word. Pauses are just as important as the words themselves. They create suspense and allow your listener to reflect on what you've said. Sometimes, it's in the moments of silence that desire builds the most.

Conversation, when seductive, is never about small talk. Dive deep, ask the questions that make people reveal who they truly are. What do they desire? What do they dream about? What keeps them awake at night? These are the things that bring out someone's innermost self, the things they rarely share with anyone else. And when someone shares their deepest desires with you, the connection becomes more than just physical—it becomes a bond of emotional intimacy.

> *"Seduction isn't just in the touch;*
> *it's in the words that leave you*
> *craving for more long after*
> *they've been spoken."*

Never rush to fill the silence. A seductive conversation is one that flows naturally, where each word builds upon the last, leading to a crescendo of intimacy that feels effortless. Compliment, but do so sparingly. Instead of focusing on the obvious—like physical appearance—compliment something more intimate: the way they think, the way they laugh, or how they make you feel in their presence. This shows that you're paying attention on a deeper level, which is incredibly seductive.

3. The Dance of Touch: Building Sensual Tension

Touch is perhaps the most powerful form of communication when it comes to seduction, but like all things in the art of seduction, it must be done with subtlety and restraint. The goal is not to overwhelm the other person with physical contact, but to create a slow burn, a build-up of sensual tension that leaves them wanting more.

Begin with the lightest, most casual of touches—a brush of your hand against theirs, your knee accidentally grazing theirs under the table, a fleeting touch on the small of their back as you guide them through a door. Each touch should feel accidental, almost unintentional, as if you're not even aware of the effect it's having. But of course, you are. Every touch should linger just long enough to create a spark, but never long enough to feel deliberate.

> *"The most seductive touch is the one that leaves you wondering if it was intentional."*

As the connection deepens, your touches can become more intimate. A hand placed gently on the back of their neck, a whisper close to their ear that allows your breath to brush against their skin. Each touch should feel like a promise of more to come, building anticipation with every interaction.

Remember, in seduction, patience is key. The longer you can draw out the process, the more powerful the eventual connection will be. The anticipation is often more thrilling than the act itself. Let the tension build naturally, without rushing toward a physical conclusion. The more time you spend creating tension, the more intense the release will be.

4. The Power of Vulnerability: Breaking Down Walls

Seduction isn't just about physical attraction; it's about creating an emotional connection. The deepest seductions are those where two people allow themselves to be vulnerable with one another, where walls are broken down, and raw emotion is laid bare.

Vulnerability is seductive because it's rare. In a world where everyone is guarded, showing someone your true self is incredibly powerful. This doesn't mean oversharing or revealing your deepest secrets all at once. Vulnerability in seduction is about letting someone see the real you—the parts of you that aren't perfect, the parts that make you human.

"True seduction lies in the moment you let someone see past the facade and into your soul."

When you open up, you invite the other person to do the same. This creates a bond that goes beyond physical attraction and taps into something deeper. Seduction becomes not just about desire, but about trust. The person you're seducing feels safe with you, and that safety is incredibly alluring.

To be vulnerable in seduction, you must be willing to listen as much as you talk. Ask the right questions, the ones that encourage the other person to open up. When they do, listen intently. Make them feel heard and understood. There is nothing more seductive than feeling like the person you're with truly sees you.

5. Escalating Intimacy: Creating Moments of Connection

As the tension builds, the intimacy between you and the person you're seducing should escalate naturally. This isn't just about physical intimacy—it's about creating moments that feel deeply personal and connected. Whether it's sharing a private joke, revealing something about your past, or simply sitting in comfortable silence, these moments of connection are what deepen the bond.

> *"Intimacy isn't about how close you get physically; it's about how close you allow yourself to be emotionally."*

Creating intimacy is about paying attention to the little things. Notice the way they hold their glass, the way they laugh, the way they fidget when they're nervous. When you notice these things, it shows that you're fully present in the moment, that you're paying attention to every detail. This kind of attentiveness is incredibly seductive.

Physical intimacy, when it happens, should feel like a natural progression of the emotional intimacy you've built. It should never feel rushed or forced. Instead, let it unfold organically, as a continuation of the connection you've already established. When physical intimacy is the result of a deep emotional connection, it becomes much more meaningful and powerful.

6. Sustaining Seduction: The Long Game

Seduction doesn't end after the first kiss or the first night together. In fact, the most powerful seductions are the ones that continue long after the initial moment of intimacy. To truly master the art of seduction, you must learn how to sustain the connection, how to keep the other person intrigued and engaged.

"Seduction is not a sprint; it's a marathon. The goal is not just to win their body, but to capture their mind and soul."

Sustaining seduction is about continuing to be present, continuing to show interest, and continuing to create moments of connection. It's about keeping the mystery alive, never revealing everything all at once. The most seductive people are the ones who always leave something to the imagination, who keep you guessing and wanting more.

Keep the communication going. Send a thoughtful text, something that reminds them of a shared moment, or a playful message that keeps the tension alive. These small gestures show that you're still thinking about them, still invested in the connection, even when you're not physically together.

7. The Seduction of Confidence and Independence

One of the most seductive qualities you can possess is independence. When you have your own life, your own passions, and your own sense of purpose, you become infinitely more attractive. Seduction is not about being needy or clingy; it's about showing the other person that you are whole on your own, but that their presence in your life makes it even better.

> *"The most seductive people are those who are*
> *content with themselves but invite others to join*
> *|them in their world."*

Confidence in your independence is a powerful tool in seduction. When the person you're seducing sees that you don't need them to complete you, but that you desire them out of genuine interest, it creates a sense of security and intrigue. They want to be a part of your world, but they also know that you are perfectly capable of thriving without them.

This kind of confidence is magnetic. It draws people in, not because you're chasing them, but because they want to be a part of the energy you radiate. They want to be close to someone who is so sure of themselves, so comfortable in their own skin.

8. Mastering Seduction: A Lifelong Journey

Seduction is not something you master overnight. It's a lifelong journey of understanding human nature, of learning how to connect with others on a deeper level, and of constantly evolving your own sense of self. To truly master the art of seduction, you must be willing to continuously grow and adapt, to learn from each encounter and to apply that knowledge to future experiences.

> *"Seduction is an art that is perfected over time,*
> *with practice, patience, and a deep understanding*
> *of human desire."*

As you continue to practice the art of seduction, remember that it's not about manipulation or control. True seduction is about connection, about creating an experience that is mutually satisfying for both you and the person you're seducing. It's about building trust, intimacy, and desire in a way that feels natural and organic.

The art of seduction is timeless. It's an essential part of human connection, a dance that has been played out for centuries and will continue to be explored for centuries to come. And while the techniques may change with time, the core principles of seduction—confidence, presence, patience, and vulnerability—will always remain.

9. Conclusion

In conclusion, seduction is not a mere physical act. It is a complex and nuanced dance of emotions, desires, and connections. It is about understanding human nature, about listening as much as you speak, about touching as much as you hold back. To seduce is to create a space where desire can grow naturally and authentically. And when done with respect, intention, and emotional intelligence, seduction becomes not just an art, but a transformative experience that lingers long after the moment has passed.

Chapter 4

The Game of Money

Understanding Money as a Game of Strategy

Money, in its essence, is a medium of exchange, a means for trading goods and services. However, when viewed through the lens of strategy, it becomes so much more than that—it becomes a tool for building wealth, security, and freedom. To master money is to understand that every financial decision is like a move in a game. Some moves are defensive, designed to protect your wealth, while others are offensive, aimed at growing it. But like any game, success requires skill, patience, and strategy.

In this detailed exploration, we will look beyond the surface of financial advice and delve into the nuances of managing money strategically. We'll discuss concepts that are often overlooked, such as the psychology of wealth, the difference between good and bad debt, the power of time in investments, the hidden traps of lifestyle inflation, and how the financial system can either work for you or against you, depending on your understanding of its mechanics. This chapter is designed to provide both a theoretical and practical framework for financial mastery—one that is comprehensive, informed, and actionable.

1. The Foundations of Financial Strategy

1. Money as a Tool, Not a Goal

One of the most important mental shifts required to succeed in the game of money is realizing that money is not the end goal. It's a tool, a means to achieve freedom, security, and the ability to live life on your terms. Many people make the mistake of thinking that money, in itself, is the goal, but this leads to shortsighted decisions driven by greed or fear. True financial success comes when you focus on using money as a tool to achieve bigger life goals.

2. The Mindset Shift: From Scarcity to Abundance

A common obstacle in achieving financial success is a scarcity mindset—the belief that there is never enough. This can lead to irrational fears about spending, or alternatively, hoarding wealth in ways that don't benefit long-term financial growth. An abundance mindset, on the other hand, focuses on the idea that there is plenty of wealth to go around and that you are capable of earning and managing more. Shifting from a scarcity to an abundance mindset doesn't mean spending recklessly; it means trusting in your ability to manage, grow, and multiply your resources over time.

2. Good Debt vs. Bad Debt: The Double-Edged Sword

Debt is often viewed as inherently negative, but it's important to differentiate between good debt and bad debt. While bad debt can indeed ruin financial stability, good debt, when used strategically, can be a powerful tool for building wealth.

1. Understanding Bad Debt

Bad debt is typically associated with consumer debt—credit cards, payday loans, and other forms of borrowing that are used to fund depreciating assets or non-essential consumption. This type of debt not only has high interest rates but also provides no return on investment. Instead, it drains future income, making it harder to save and invest. If you're paying 20% interest on credit card debt, that's 20% of your potential investment returns disappearing each month.

Example: If you charge $5,000 to a credit card with a 20% interest rate and only make the minimum payments, it could take you years to pay off the balance, and you'll end up paying thousands more in interest. This debt does nothing to improve your financial position and only serves to enrich the lender.

2. Leveraging Good Debt

Good debt, on the other hand, is debt that helps you acquire assets that appreciate over time, such as real estate, education, or a business. For example, a mortgage on a rental property can be considered good debt if the property generates income and appreciates in value over time. Similarly, a loan to fund education that significantly increases your earning potential is also considered good debt.

Example: Taking a $200,000 mortgage on a property that appreciates at 5% per year and generates rental income can help you build wealth, as the property's value grows, and the income covers the cost of the mortgage.

The key to leveraging good debt is to ensure that the return on your investment is greater than the cost of borrowing. If you're borrowing money at 4% interest and earning an 8% return on that investment, you're effectively profiting from the debt.

"Not all debt is bad; it's how you use it that determines whether it builds wealth or erodes it."

3. The Psychology of Wealth: How Mindset Affects Financial Success

Money is as much a psychological game as it is a strategic one. Your beliefs, emotions, and habits around money can have a significant impact on your financial success. Understanding the psychological aspect of money is critical for making sound financial decisions.

1. Emotional Spending

One of the most common financial pitfalls is emotional spending. This occurs when you use money as a way to cope with stress, boredom, or other emotions. While it may provide temporary relief, emotional spending often leads to financial problems in the long term.

Example: Someone who has a stressful job might buy expensive clothes or gadgets to make themselves feel better, only to regret the purchases later when the credit card bill arrives. This type of spending is impulsive and not aligned with long-term financial goals.

2. Fear of Investing

Many people, especially those who grew up in financially unstable households, develop a fear of investing. They may hoard their money in savings accounts, believing that the stock market is too risky or that they're not capable of understanding it. This fear of investing can prevent them from building wealth over time, as inflation erodes the value of their savings.

Example: Keeping $50,000 in a savings account that earns 0.5% interest may feel safe, but over time, inflation will reduce its purchasing power. Investing that money in a diversified portfolio, on the other hand, could generate higher returns and protect against inflation.

The solution to these psychological barriers is self-awareness and education. By understanding your financial habits and learning more about investing, you can develop healthier relationships with money and make decisions that align with your long-term goals.

"Wealth is not just about how much money you have; it's about how you manage it and the mindset you bring to your financial decisions."

4. Investing: The Power of Compound Growth and Long-Term Thinking

Investing is one of the most powerful tools for building wealth, yet it's often misunderstood or underutilized. Many people avoid investing because they see it as risky or complicated, but with the right strategy, investing can provide consistent, long-term growth.

1. The Power of Compound Interest

Albert Einstein famously referred to compound interest as the "eighth wonder of the world." The principle is simple: when you invest money, you earn interest not only on your initial investment but also on the interest that accumulates over time. This creates a snowball effect, where your wealth grows faster and faster the longer you leave it invested.

Example: If you invest $10,000 at a 7% annual return, after 10 years, your investment will grow to approximately $19,671. After 20 years, it will grow to $38,696, and after 30 years, it will grow to $76,123. The longer you leave your money invested, the more it compounds.

This is why time in the market is more important than timing the market. The earlier you start investing, the more time your money has to grow.

2. The Risks of Bad Investing

While investing can build wealth, poor investment choices can quickly erode it. One of the biggest mistakes people make is chasing short-term gains, often by investing in speculative assets or "hot" stocks without doing proper research. This can lead to significant losses, as markets are volatile, and speculative investments can crash as quickly as they rise.

Example: Many people who invested in cryptocurrency during its peak in 2017 saw massive losses when the market crashed in 2018. Similarly, investors who chase "penny stocks" often lose money because these stocks are highly volatile and not backed by solid financials.

To avoid the pitfalls of bad investing, it's important to diversify your portfolio and focus on long-term growth rather than short-term gains. Diversification spreads risk across different asset classes, such as stocks, bonds, and real estate, which helps protect your portfolio from market volatility.

"Investing should be more like watching paint dry or grass grow. If you want excitement, take $800 and go to Las Vegas." – Paul Samuelson

5. The Hidden Dangers of Lifestyle Inflation

One of the most insidious challenges in managing money is lifestyle inflation. This occurs when your income increases, and instead of saving or investing the extra money, you spend it on upgrading your lifestyle. While it may feel good in the short term, lifestyle inflation can prevent you from building long-term wealth.

1. The Trap of "Keeping Up with the Joneses"

Social pressure often plays a significant role in lifestyle inflation. When you see your friends or colleagues buying new cars, moving into bigger homes, or going on expensive vacations, it's easy to feel like you need to do the same to keep up. However, this type of spending is often unsustainable and leads to living paycheck to paycheck, regardless of how much you earn.

Example: A person who earns $50,000 per year and saves 20% of their income is in a better financial position than someone who earns $100,000 but spends all of it on luxury items. The first person is building wealth, while the second is just maintaining their lifestyle without accumulating any assets.

2. How to Avoid Lifestyle Inflation

The key to avoiding lifestyle inflation is to increase your savings and investments in proportion to your income. As your income grows, you should also grow your wealth by directing a percentage of it toward investments and savings rather than spending it all on material goods.

Example: If you receive a $10,000 raise, instead of upgrading your car or moving to a more expensive apartment, you could invest that extra money in stocks, bonds, or real estate, allowing it to grow over time and contribute to your long-term financial security.

*"It's not your salary that makes you rich;
it's your spending habits."*

*"It's not your salary that makes you rich;
it's your spending habits."*

6. Risk Management: Protecting Your Wealth

While growing wealth is important, it's equally important to protect it. Risk management involves safeguarding your assets from unexpected events that could derail your financial plans.

1. Insurance as a Safety Net

Insurance is one of the most effective ways to manage financial risk. Whether it's health insurance, life insurance, or homeowner's insurance, having the right coverage can protect you from financial ruin in the event of a crisis.

Example: A person without health insurance who has a medical emergency could be faced with tens of thousands of dollars in medical bills, which could wipe out their savings and leave them in debt. On the other hand, someone with insurance can mitigate these costs and protect their financial future.

2. Emergency Funds: Your First Line of Defense

An emergency fund is another critical component of risk management. This is a cash reserve set aside to cover unexpected expenses, such as medical bills, car repairs, or job loss. An emergency fund provides a buffer, so you don't have to rely on credit cards or loans to cover these costs, which could lead to debt.

Example: Financial experts recommend having three to six months' worth of living expenses saved in an emergency fund. This ensures that you can cover essential expenses without going into debt if an unexpected event occurs.

7. The Importance of Financial Education: Knowledge is Power

One of the most overlooked aspects of financial strategy is education. In today's complex financial landscape, understanding how money works is crucial for making informed decisions. Unfortunately, many people lack basic financial literacy, which can lead to poor financial choices and prevent them from achieving long-term success.

1. Continuous Learning: Staying Informed

The financial world is constantly evolving, with new investment opportunities, tax laws, and economic trends emerging regularly. To stay ahead of the game, it's important to continuously educate yourself about personal finance. This can be done through reading books, attending seminars, or following financial experts.

Example: Someone who learned about the benefits of index fund investing in the early 2000s and started investing consistently would likely have seen significant returns over the past two decades. On the other hand, someone who didn't stay informed may have missed out on these opportunities.

2. Avoiding Financial Scams and Pitfalls

Financial scams are becoming increasingly sophisticated, and without proper education, it's easy to fall victim to them. Whether it's a Ponzi scheme, a phishing email, or a too-good-to-be-true investment opportunity, scammers prey on those who lack financial knowledge.

Example: In the early 2000s, many investors fell victim to Bernie Madoff's Ponzi scheme, losing billions of dollars. Understanding basic financial principles, such as the importance of diversification and skepticism of unusually high returns, could have helped investors avoid these losses.

"An investment in knowledge pays the best interest." – Benjamin Franklin

8. Conclusion: Mastering the Game of Money

The game of money is one that requires strategy, discipline, and patience. By understanding the difference between good and bad debt, managing your emotions around money, leveraging the power of compound interest, avoiding lifestyle inflation, and continuously educating yourself, you can achieve long-term financial success.

The key is to view money not as the ultimate goal but as a tool for building the life you want. With the right mindset, strategy, and knowledge, you can take control of your financial future and play the game of money to win.

Budgeting and Saving: The Defensive Strategy

In the world of personal finance, budgeting and saving are your defensive plays. Just as in a game of strategy, a strong defense ensures that you are able to protect your financial resources, cover your immediate needs, and prepare for unexpected setbacks. Without these defenses, it becomes far too easy to lose your hard-earned money and fall into financial disarray. Budgeting is not about restriction, but about freedom—the freedom to spend wisely, save effectively, and invest purposefully.

Budgeting and saving are the tools you use to ensure your financial goals are met, that emergencies do not spiral into disasters, and that the things that matter most in life—whether it be a home, education, or even travel—are achievable. In this chapter, we'll explore the different components of budgeting and saving, provide detailed examples of how they work in practice, and dive deep into common financial pitfalls that often trip people up on their way to financial security. We will also explore how budgeting and saving can lead to not just financial security, but financial independence, which ultimately gives you the freedom to pursue your life's goals with peace of mind.

1. The Role of Budgeting: Controlling Your Financial Destiny

Understanding the Purpose of Budgeting

At its most basic, a budget is a plan for how you will allocate your money. It is a roadmap to ensure that your income is properly directed towards things that matter—needs, wants, savings, and investments—rather than vanishing into impulsive purchases or unplanned expenses. But a budget is more than just a planning tool; it is a means of empowering yourself to make deliberate, thoughtful financial decisions.

Many people mistakenly believe that budgeting is a restrictive or joyless task, where you deprive yourself of pleasures in the name of saving. However, a well-planned budget is actually quite the opposite. Rather than restricting your choices, it allows you to spend freely within the parameters that ensure financial health. It is about controlling your money, rather than letting your money control you.

Budgeting is about aligning your financial choices with your personal goals. This could be saving for a down payment on a house, planning for a child's education, preparing for retirement, or simply eliminating the stress of living paycheck to paycheck. Without a budget, you are essentially flying blind, reacting to financial situations as they arise instead of planning for them. This reactive financial behavior leads to overspending, debt, and a lack of savings, leaving many people in a constant state of financial anxiety.

A budget, therefore, serves as the cornerstone of your financial plan, setting the stage for financial security and prosperity.

Creating a Realistic and Flexible Budget

There are many different methods for creating a budget, but one of the most commonly used and effective is the **50/30/20 rule**. This method divides your after-tax income into three main categories:

50% for necessities: These include essential expenses such as housing, utilities, groceries, insurance, and transportation. These are non-negotiable, everyday needs that must be covered to maintain a basic standard of living.

30% for discretionary spending: This portion is reserved for things that you want but don't necessarily need—such as dining out, entertainment, hobbies, or travel. It allows you to enjoy life's pleasures without going overboard.

20% for savings and debt repayment: This portion of your income is dedicated to building your financial future, which includes saving for emergencies, investing for retirement, and paying down any debts.

The simplicity of this method is part of its power. It provides a straightforward framework that allows for flexibility in how you allocate your money while ensuring that your savings and financial future are given proper priority. However, every individual or family is different, and the 50/30/20 rule can be adjusted based on personal circumstances. For instance, if you have significant debt, you may allocate more than 20% of your income toward paying it off. Or, if you have lower fixed expenses, you may choose to save more aggressively.

Imagine you earn $5,000 per month after taxes. Under the 50/30/20 rule:

$2,500 goes to needs such as rent, groceries, utilities, and transportation.

$1,500 goes to discretionary spending like entertainment, dining out, and vacations.

$1,000 goes into savings, investments, or toward paying off debt.

With this structure, you avoid the trap of living beyond your means. You're saving for the future, enjoying life in the present, and ensuring that your basic needs are covered.

2. Understanding the Psychology of Spending

Emotional Spending and Its Triggers

Spending isn't just a rational act; it's often emotional. We don't always spend because we need something, or even because we want it. Often, we spend because we're bored, stressed, or seeking a quick emotional boost. This is known as **emotional spending**. When we're stressed, for example, buying something new might give us a temporary high, but in the long run, it can lead to buyer's remorse, guilt, and financial strain.

This behavior is driven by the reward centers of the brain. Spending money, particularly on discretionary items like clothes, gadgets, or luxury items, can release dopamine—a feel-good neurotransmitter. Unfortunately, this high is short-lived, and we often end up feeling worse, especially if the spending was impulsive or unnecessary.

The key to overcoming emotional spending is recognizing your triggers. Do you tend to shop when you're feeling anxious or lonely? Are there certain environments (such as malls or online marketplaces) that tempt you to spend more than you should? Once you identify your spending triggers, you can create strategies to avoid them, such as setting a 24-hour waiting period before making non-essential purchases or finding alternative ways to cope with negative emotions, such as exercising or talking to a friend.

Impulse Buying vs. Thoughtful Spending

Impulse buying is one of the main reasons people blow through their budgets. Whether it's picking up items near the checkout line or making a spur-of-the-moment purchase online, impulse buying is often fueled by emotions rather than necessity. A simple way to curb this behavior is to follow the **"24-hour rule"**—if you see something you want, wait 24 hours before purchasing it. This gives you time to think about whether the purchase is necessary or just a momentary desire.

Additionally, setting clear goals for your spending can help. If you know you're saving for a big purchase—such as a vacation, a new car, or a house—it becomes easier to resist the temptation to buy smaller, unnecessary items. Every time you refrain from making an impulse purchase, you're one step closer to achieving your financial goals.

Let's say you're browsing an online store and see a pair of expensive shoes that you don't really need but feel tempted to buy. Instead of clicking "buy now," you wait 24 hours. In that time, you might realize that you already have enough shoes or that the money would be better spent on something else. By delaying the purchase, you're able to make a more thoughtful decision and avoid unnecessary spending.

3. Building an Emergency Fund: Preparing for the Unexpected

Why an Emergency Fund is Essential

An emergency fund is your financial safety net. It's money set aside to cover unexpected expenses, such as medical bills, car repairs, or job loss. Without an emergency fund, these unexpected expenses can throw your entire financial plan off course, leading to debt, stress, and financial instability.

Financial experts generally recommend having at least three to six months' worth of living expenses saved in an easily accessible account. This ensures that if you face an unexpected financial crisis, you have enough money to cover your basic needs without resorting to credit cards or loans, which can lead to high interest rates and long-term debt.

How to Build an Emergency Fund

The key to building an emergency fund is consistency. Start by setting a specific goal for how much you want to save and then automate your savings. By setting up automatic transfers from your checking account to a dedicated savings account, you ensure that a portion of your income is saved each month without having to think about it.

A high-yield savings account is often the best place to keep your emergency fund. It's easily accessible in case of an emergency, but it also earns interest, so your money is growing while it's sitting in the bank. However, the primary goal of an emergency fund is not to earn high returns, but to provide liquidity and safety.

Let's say your monthly living expenses (rent, utilities, groceries, etc.) total $3,000. You should aim to have between $9,000 and $18,000 saved in your emergency fund. This money would be used only for true emergencies, such as unexpected medical expenses or losing your job. By having this safety net, you're able to navigate life's uncertainties without the added stress of financial instability.

4. Automating Your Savings: The Easiest Way to Save

The Benefits of Automated Savings

Automating your savings is one of the most effective ways to build wealth over time. When you automate your savings, you set up recurring transfers from your checking account to your savings or investment accounts. This ensures that you're consistently saving money without the temptation to spend it.

The beauty of automation is that it removes the need for willpower. You don't have to rely on your own discipline to set aside money each month—it happens automatically. By treating your savings like any other fixed expense, such as rent or utilities, you make it a non-negotiable part of your financial plan.

Many employers offer automatic payroll deductions, allowing you to direct a portion of your paycheck into a savings or retirement account before it even hits your checking account. This "pay yourself first" approach ensures that you're saving for your future before you have a chance to spend the money on other things.

Example:

Let's say you want to save $500 per month. By setting up an automatic transfer from your checking account to your savings account, you ensure that this money is saved before you have a chance to spend it. Over time, this consistent savings habit will help you build wealth and achieve your financial goals.

5. Debt: A Double-Edged Sword

The Danger of High-Interest Debt

Debt is a reality for many people, but not all debt is created equal. High-interest debt, such as credit card debt or payday loans, can quickly spiral out of control. The interest rates on these types of loans are often so high that even making the minimum payments barely covers the interest, leaving the principal amount untouched.

If you're carrying high-interest debt, it's essential to prioritize paying it off as quickly as possible. The longer you carry this debt, the more it will cost you in interest payments, which can severely limit your ability to save, invest, and achieve your financial goals.

One effective strategy for paying off high-interest debt is the **debt avalanche method**. With this approach, you focus on paying off your debt with the highest interest rate first, while making minimum payments on your other debts. Once the highest-interest debt is paid off, you move on to the next highest, and so on. This method saves you the most money in interest payments over time.

Let's say you have three credit cards with balances of $2,000, $3,000, and $5,000, with interest rates of 18%, 15%, and 10%, respectively. Under the debt avalanche method, you would focus on paying off the $2,000 balance first, as it has the highest interest rate. Once that debt is paid off, you move on to the next highest-interest debt, and so on.

By using this strategy, you're able to minimize the amount of interest you pay, which allows you to pay off your debt faster and free up money for savings and investments.

6. Good Debt vs. Bad Debt: Knowing the Difference

Not all debt is bad. Some types of debt can actually help you build wealth over time. For example, taking out a mortgage to buy a home or borrowing money to invest in your education can be considered "good debt" because these investments have the potential to increase your net worth in the long run.

However, it's important to be strategic about how much debt you take on and to ensure that you're able to manage it responsibly. Just because a loan is for a "good" purpose doesn't mean it's automatically a smart financial move. You still need to consider factors such as interest rates, repayment terms, and your overall financial situation.

Good Debt includes:

Mortgages: A home is often considered an investment because it typically appreciates in value over time. Additionally, mortgage interest rates are generally lower than other types of loans, and the interest is tax-deductible in many cases.

Student Loans: Borrowing money to invest in your education can pay off in the long run, as higher education often leads to higher earning potential. However, it's important to borrow responsibly and to be mindful of the repayment terms.

Bad Debt includes:

Credit Card Debt: Credit cards often come with high-interest rates, and carrying a balance can quickly become expensive. If you're not able to pay off your balance in full each month, you're likely paying more in interest than the value of the items you purchased.

Payday Loans: Payday loans are notorious for their exorbitant interest rates and fees, making them one of the most dangerous types of debt. These loans should be avoided at all costs.

By understanding the difference between good and bad debt, you can make informed decisions about when it makes sense to borrow money and when it's better to avoid taking on debt altogether.

7. Conclusion: Mastering the Defensive Game

Budgeting and saving are the foundation of financial security. By creating a realistic budget, controlling emotional spending, building an emergency fund, and automating your savings, you can develop the financial discipline needed to achieve long-term success.

Remember, the key to winning the game of money is not just about how much you earn but how wisely you manage and protect what you have. With the right defensive strategies in place, you can build a strong financial foundation that will support you through life's ups and downs.

> *"A budget is telling your money where*
> *to go instead of wondering where it went."*
> *– Dave Ramsey*

Investing: The Offensive Strategy

In the financial game of life, investing is your offensive strategy. While budgeting and saving act as your defense, helping you preserve your wealth, investing allows you to grow that wealth, making your money work harder for you. Whether you're saving for retirement, a child's education, or a large purchase, investing is the most effective way to build wealth over time.

Investing isn't just for the rich; it's a game that anyone can play with the right strategies, mindset, and discipline. When done thoughtfully, investing can turn small amounts of money into significant wealth, and it allows you to take advantage of compound interest, market growth, and financial opportunities that go beyond simply saving money in a bank.

In this chapter, we'll explore the key principles of investing, the different types of investments available, how to assess risk, and strategies to optimize your investments for long-term success. You'll also learn how to avoid common mistakes that derail many investors, and how to build a portfolio that aligns with your financial goals.

1. The Importance of Investing: Why It's Essential for Wealth Building

Why Investing Beats Saving

One of the most important financial truths is that **saving alone will not make you wealthy**. While saving money is crucial for short-term financial goals and emergencies, it doesn't offer the same potential for growth that investing does. In fact, keeping too much money in a savings account can actually cost you due to inflation.

Inflation is the gradual increase in prices over time, which erodes the purchasing power of money. If inflation averages 2-3% per year and your savings account earns less than that (which most do), then the value of your money decreases over time. In other words, you're actually losing money in real terms by keeping it in a low-interest savings account.

Investing, on the other hand, offers the potential for returns that outpace inflation. Historically, the stock market has provided an average return of about 7-10% per year, far higher than what any savings account offers. By investing, you're not just preserving your wealth—you're growing it.

Compounding: The Eighth Wonder of the World

One of the most powerful concepts in investing is **compound interest**. This occurs when the returns you earn on an investment are reinvested, allowing you to earn returns on your initial investment as well as on the returns themselves. Over time, this leads to exponential growth.

For example, if you invest $10,000 at an average annual return of 7%, after 10 years, your investment would grow to approximately $19,671. If you leave it invested for 20 years, it would grow to $38,697.

The longer you leave your money invested, the more you benefit from compounding.

This is why it's so important to start investing early. The more time you give your money to grow, the greater your potential returns. Even small, regular contributions to an investment account can grow into a substantial sum over time.

Example:

If you start investing $200 per month at the age of 25 and earn an average return of 7%, by the time you're 65, you'll have approximately $525,000. However, if you wait until age 35 to start investing the same amount, you'll only have about $244,000 by age 65. The extra 10 years of investing can more than double your final balance due to the power of compounding.

2. Types of Investments: Understanding Your Options

Investing is not a one-size-fits-all strategy. There are many different types of investments, each with its own risk level, potential return, and time horizon. To build a strong investment portfolio, it's important to understand the various options available to you and how they fit into your overall financial plan.

Stocks: Ownership in Companies

When you buy a **stock**, you are purchasing a share of ownership in a company. Stocks are one of the most common and accessible forms of investment and historically have offered some of the highest returns over the long term. However, they also come with higher risk compared to other types of investments.

Stocks can be divided into two main categories:

Individual Stocks: These are shares in specific companies, such as Apple, Amazon, or Tesla. Investing in individual stocks can be highly profitable if the company performs well, but it also carries the risk of significant losses if the company struggles.

Index Funds and ETFs: Rather than picking individual stocks, many investors choose to invest in index funds or exchange-traded funds (ETFs), which track the performance of a broad market index, such as the S&P 500. These funds offer diversification (spreading your risk across many companies) and tend to be less risky than individual stocks while still offering strong long-term returns.

Bonds: Lending Money to Earn Interest

When you invest in a **bond**, you are essentially lending money to a government or corporation in exchange for regular interest payments and the return of your principal when the bond matures. Bonds are considered lower risk than stocks, but they also offer lower potential returns.

There are several types of bonds:

Government Bonds: These are issued by national governments and are considered very safe, especially in stable countries like the U.S. Treasury bonds, for example, are backed by the full faith and credit of the U.S. government.

Corporate Bonds: These are issued by companies and typically offer higher interest rates than government bonds because they come with more risk.

Real Estate: A Tangible Asset

Investing in **real estate** involves buying property—whether it's a home, an apartment building, or commercial space—with the expectation that it will increase in value over time or generate rental income. Real estate can provide a steady stream of income, especially if you invest in rental properties, but it also requires significant upfront capital and ongoing maintenance.

Real estate is also considered a relatively illiquid investment, meaning it can take time to sell if you need to access your money quickly. However, many investors find that real estate is a valuable part of a diversified portfolio due to its potential for growth and income generation.

Mutual Funds: Professionally Managed Portfolios

Mutual funds are a type of investment where money from many investors is pooled together and managed by a professional investment manager. The manager invests the money in a diversified portfolio of stocks, bonds, or other assets. Mutual funds offer investors the benefit of professional management and diversification but typically come with higher fees than index funds or ETFs.

Alternative Investments: Risk and Reward

In addition to stocks, bonds, and real estate, there are a variety of **alternative investments** that can offer high returns but come with increased risk. These include:

Cryptocurrency: Digital currencies like Bitcoin and Ethereum have gained popularity in recent years as an alternative investment. However, they are extremely volatile and speculative, so they should be approached with caution.

Commodities: Investing in commodities such as gold, oil, or agricultural products can provide a hedge against inflation and market volatility, but these markets can be unpredictable and challenging to navigate.

Private Equity: Investing in private companies can offer significant returns if the company grows, but it also comes with high risk, as many startups fail.

3. Risk Management: Protecting Your Investments

Understanding Risk vs. Reward

Every investment comes with a certain level of **risk**, and understanding how to manage that risk is crucial to being a successful investor. Generally, the higher the potential return on an investment, the higher the risk. Conversely, safer investments like bonds tend to offer lower returns.

One of the keys to managing risk is finding the right balance between risk and reward based on your financial goals, time horizon, and risk tolerance. A younger investor with a long time horizon can afford to take on more risk because they have time to recover from market downturns. On the other hand, an investor nearing retirement may prefer more conservative investments to protect their wealth.

Diversification: Don't Put All Your Eggs in One Basket

One of the most effective ways to manage risk is through **diversification**—the practice of spreading your investments across different asset classes (stocks, bonds, real estate, etc.) and industries. By diversifying, you reduce the impact of any one investment's poor performance on your overall portfolio.

For example, if you invest all your money in technology stocks and the tech sector experiences a downturn, your entire portfolio could suffer significant losses. However, if you diversify your investments across different industries (e.g., healthcare, finance, energy) and asset classes, a downturn in one sector will have less impact on your overall portfolio.

Rebalancing: Keeping Your Portfolio on Track

Over time, the value of your investments will fluctuate, and your portfolio may become unbalanced. For example, if the stock market has a strong year, the percentage of your portfolio invested in stocks may become larger than your original allocation. To maintain your desired level of risk, it's important to periodically **rebalance** your portfolio—meaning you sell some of your overperforming assets and reinvest the proceeds in underperforming ones.

Rebalancing ensures that you're not taking on more risk than you intended and helps you stick to your long-term investment strategy.

4. Investing for the Long Term: Patience and Discipline

The Value of a Long-Term Perspective

Investing is not a get-rich-quick scheme. The most successful investors are those who take a **long-term approach**, staying patient and disciplined even when markets are volatile. Trying to time the market—buying when stocks are low and selling when they're high—often leads to poor decision-making and subpar returns.

The stock market will always have ups and downs, but historically, it has trended upward over the long term. By staying invested and resisting the urge to sell during market downturns, you give your investments the time they need to recover and grow.

The Danger of Emotional Investing

One of the biggest mistakes investors make is letting their emotions dictate their investment decisions. When the market is doing well, it's easy to get caught up in the excitement and invest more money than you should. Conversely, when the market is down, fear and panic can lead you to sell your investments at a loss.

To avoid emotional investing, it's important to stick to your investment plan and remember that **volatility is a normal part of the market**. If you've built a diversified portfolio and are investing for the long term, short-term market fluctuations shouldn't affect your overall strategy.

Example:

During the 2008 financial crisis, many investors panicked and sold their stocks when the market dropped. However, those who stayed invested and continued to contribute to their portfolios were rewarded when the market eventually recovered and went on to reach new highs.

5. Avoiding Common Investing Mistakes

Chasing Performance

One of the most common investing mistakes is **chasing performance**—buying into investments that have recently performed well, assuming that they will continue to do so. However, past performance is not indicative of future results, and by the time an investment has performed well enough to catch your attention, much of the growth may have already occurred.

A better approach is to focus on investments that are aligned with your financial goals and risk tolerance, rather than trying to pick the "hot" investment of the moment.

Failing to Research Investments

Another common mistake is failing to do proper research before investing. It's easy to be swayed by a friend's recommendation or a news article about the latest investment trend, but it's important to understand exactly what you're investing in and why.

Before making any investment, take the time to research the company, fund, or asset class thoroughly. Understand its risks, potential returns, and how it fits into your overall portfolio.

6. Conclusion: Playing Offense with Your Investments

Investing is the most powerful offensive strategy in the game of money. By understanding the different types of investments available, managing risk effectively, and taking a long-term approach, you can grow your wealth and achieve your financial goals. Remember, investing is not just about making money—it's about building a secure financial future and creating opportunities for yourself and your loved ones.

"The stock market is a device for transferring money from the impatient to the patient."
— Warren Buffett

The Importance of Financial Discipline

Financial discipline is often seen as the backbone of personal finance management. Without it, even the best strategies for budgeting, saving, and investing can fall apart. It is what helps you stay on track toward achieving financial goals, ensuring that you don't fall prey to short-term temptations or emotional decisions that can derail your long-term success.

In this chapter, we will dive into the concept of financial discipline, exploring why it is essential, how it applies to various aspects of money management, and how you can develop and maintain discipline in your financial life. The goal is to provide a holistic understanding that allows you to align your behaviors with your financial goals and make better decisions in the face of life's financial challenges.

1. What Is Financial Discipline?

Financial discipline refers to the practice of consistently managing your money in a way that aligns with your financial goals. It involves making thoughtful and often difficult decisions about how you earn, spend, save, and invest your money. Discipline isn't just about saying no to the things you want; it's about being mindful of your long-term goals and understanding that financial success often requires sacrifice, patience, and persistence.

Key Aspects of Financial Discipline

Spending Wisely: Financial discipline means avoiding impulsive purchases and sticking to a budget, even when it's tempting to spend on non-essentials.

Saving Consistently: It's not just about saving when you have extra cash; it's about making savings a priority, even during lean times. Consistency is key.

Investing Responsibly: This includes doing thorough research before making investments, sticking to your strategy, and resisting the urge to chase short-term gains.

Managing Debt: Financial discipline involves avoiding unnecessary debt and responsibly managing any debt you do take on, ensuring that it doesn't spiral out of control.

Patience and Long-Term Focus: Successful wealth-building strategies take time, and disciplined individuals understand that patience is crucial to seeing long-term results.

2. Why Financial Discipline Is Essential

The Link Between Discipline and Financial Freedom

Financial discipline is crucial because it's directly tied to financial freedom. Without discipline, it's easy to become trapped in a cycle of debt, overspending, and financial stress. With discipline, however, you can steadily work towards achieving financial independence, where your money works for you, and you are no longer reliant on paycheck-to-paycheck living.

Imagine financial discipline as the vehicle that takes you to financial freedom. Without a strong engine (discipline), the vehicle won't move forward, and you'll stay stuck in the same place, no matter how much money you make. Whether you're earning a modest income or bringing in a six-figure salary, without discipline, wealth can easily slip through your fingers.

The Impact of Undisciplined Spending

Lack of financial discipline often manifests in undisciplined spending. This can lead to living beyond your means, accumulating high-interest debt, and eventually finding yourself in a financial hole that's difficult to escape. Credit card debt, for example, is one of the biggest consequences of undisciplined spending. Many people fall into the trap of using credit for things they can't afford, only to find themselves paying more in interest than the value of the item itself.

A survey by the Federal Reserve found that the average U.S. household carries about $6,000 in credit card debt. This is a direct consequence of a lack of financial discipline, and it's a reminder that even small, seemingly harmless purchases can add up to significant financial burdens over time.

Example:

Consider someone who habitually eats out every day, spending $20 per meal. Over a year, that adds up to $7,300—money that could have been saved, invested, or used to pay off debt. This is the power of financial discipline: recognizing where small changes can lead to big improvements in your financial life.

3. Developing Financial Discipline: Practical Steps

Developing financial discipline doesn't happen overnight. It requires building good habits, creating a plan, and sticking to it. Below are practical steps to help you cultivate discipline in managing your finances.

Step 1: Create a Budget and Stick to It

The first and most important step in developing financial discipline is creating a budget. A budget is a plan for how you'll allocate your income across different categories, including savings, expenses, and investments. It provides a roadmap that helps you manage your money intentionally, ensuring that you're not spending more than you earn.

Identify Your Income: Start by listing all sources of income, including salary, side gigs, and any other earnings.

Track Your Expenses: Identify fixed expenses (rent, utilities, loans) and variable expenses (groceries, entertainment, dining out). This will give you a clear picture of where your money is going.

Set Spending Limits: Allocate a portion of your income to each category and stick to those limits. Use tools like budgeting apps or spreadsheets to help monitor your progress.

Review and Adjust Regularly: Your budget shouldn't be static. Review it regularly to see where you might need to make adjustments based on changes in income or expenses.

Step 2: Prioritize Saving

Financial discipline involves making savings a priority, not an afterthought. The key is to pay yourself first, meaning that you should allocate a portion of your income to savings before spending on other things.

Automate Your Savings: Set up automatic transfers to a savings account as soon as your paycheck comes in. This ensures that saving becomes a habit and doesn't rely on your willpower.

Set Clear Savings Goals: Whether it's building an emergency fund, saving for a down payment, or funding your retirement, having specific savings goals will keep you motivated.

Step 3: Control Impulsive Spending

Impulse purchases can quickly derail your financial plans. Practicing restraint in your spending is a key aspect of financial discipline.

The 30-Day Rule: When tempted to make a non-essential purchase, give yourself 30 days to think about it. Often, the urge to buy fades, and you'll find that you didn't really need the item after all.

Mindful Spending: Be conscious of emotional triggers that lead to impulsive purchases. For example, many people spend money as a way to cope with stress or boredom. Recognize these patterns and find healthier ways to manage your emotions.

Step 4: Limit Your Use of Credit Cards

Credit cards can be a useful tool when managed responsibly, but they also come with the risk of debt if not used with discipline.

Use Cash or Debit Instead: One way to limit credit card debt is to use cash or debit for everyday purchases. This helps you avoid accumulating balances that you can't pay off in full.

Pay Off Balances Monthly: If you do use a credit card, commit to paying off the balance in full each month to avoid interest charges.

Step 5: Set Long-Term Financial Goals

Without long-term goals, it's easy to fall into the trap of living for today and neglecting your future. Financial discipline involves thinking beyond the present and setting goals that will improve your financial situation over time.

Retirement Savings: Contribute to retirement accounts like 401(k)s or IRAs. The earlier you start, the more time your money has to grow through compound interest.

Invest in Your Future: Whether it's buying a home, starting a business, or funding your children's education, having a long-term financial vision will give you the discipline to make smart choices now.

4. Financial Discipline in Investing

Just as discipline is important in managing your daily finances, it's equally crucial when it comes to investing. Successful investing requires a long-term mindset, patience, and the ability to avoid making emotional decisions based on short-term market fluctuations.

Avoiding Emotional Investing

One of the biggest challenges in investing is the temptation to react emotionally to market movements. When the stock market is doing well, it's easy to get caught up in the excitement and invest more money than you should. Conversely, when the market is down, fear and panic can lead you to sell your investments at a loss.

Disciplined investors understand that **volatility is a normal part of the market**. They stay focused on their long-term strategy and resist the urge to make impulsive decisions based on short-term market trends.

The Importance of Consistency in Investing

Consistency is key to successful investing. Rather than trying to time the market, disciplined investors make regular contributions to their investment accounts, regardless of market conditions. This strategy, known as **dollar-cost averaging**, involves investing a fixed amount of money at regular intervals, which reduces the risk of making poor decisions based on market timing.

Example:

Let's say you invest $500 per month in the stock market. Some months, the market will be up, and your $500 will buy fewer shares. Other months, the market will be down, and your $500 will buy more shares. Over time, this strategy helps smooth out the effects of market volatility, ensuring that you don't buy too high or sell too low.

5. The Role of Financial Discipline in Debt Management

Debt can be a useful financial tool when managed responsibly, but it can also become a major obstacle to achieving financial goals if not kept in check. Financial discipline is essential when it comes to managing debt effectively.

Good Debt vs. Bad Debt

Not all debt is created equal. **Good debt** is debt that can help you build wealth or improve your financial situation over time. For example, a mortgage on a home that appreciates in value or a student loan for a degree that increases your earning potential can be considered good debt.

Bad debt, on the other hand, is debt that doesn't provide any long-term benefit and often comes with high-interest rates. Credit card debt, payday loans, and other forms of consumer debt are examples of bad debt that can quickly spiral out of control if not managed with discipline.

Strategies for Managing Debt

Prioritize High-Interest Debt: If you have multiple debts, focus on paying off the ones with the highest interest rates first. This will save you money in the long run by reducing the amount of interest you pay.

Avoid Taking on New Debt: While you're working to pay off existing debt, avoid taking on new debt unless it's absolutely necessary. This will help you stay focused on reducing your debt load rather than adding to it.

6. Building Financial Discipline Over Time

Financial discipline is not something that develops overnight; it's a skill that you cultivate over time. The more you practice discipline in your financial life, the easier it becomes to make smart decisions that align with your long-term goals.

Accountability and Support

One way to strengthen your financial discipline is by seeking accountability and support from others. This could be a financial advisor, a trusted friend or family member, or even an online community of people working toward similar goals.

Tracking Your Progress

Another effective strategy is to track your progress over time. Keep a record of your savings, investments, and debt payments to see how far you've come. Seeing tangible progress can motivate you to stay disciplined and continue working toward your goals.

7. Conclusion: Financial Discipline as the Key to Success

Financial discipline is the foundation upon which all other aspects of personal finance are built. Whether you're budgeting, saving, investing, or managing debt, discipline ensures that you stay on track and make decisions that support your long-term financial health.

By developing and maintaining financial discipline, you can achieve your financial goals, build wealth, and ultimately attain the financial freedom that so many people strive for but few truly achieve.

"The price of anything is the
amount of life you exchange for it."
– Henry David Thoreau

Life as the Ultimate Game

Life is a lot like a game—a deeply intricate, multifaceted experience that combines strategy, resilience, knowledge, and emotional depth. However, unlike typical games, it doesn't come with a clear set of rules or an obvious path. You must learn as you go, grow through your experiences, and refine your strategies with each new challenge. At times, you may feel like you're winning; other times, like you're struggling to keep up.

The metaphor of life as a game provides an intriguing perspective on how we live. It helps us see that while we may not be able to control all the circumstances that come our way, we have the power to shape our responses, make strategic moves, and find meaning in both the wins and the losses. The goal isn't just about reaching the end successfully but about playing the game in a way that makes your life rich and purposeful.

In this chapter, we'll dive deep into the concept of life as a game, breaking it down into its essential elements—rules, strategies, challenges, and rewards. We'll explore what it takes to play the game well, how to adapt when life throws curveballs, and why the journey is more important than the destination. Whether you're just starting out in adulthood, navigating mid-life, or reflecting in later years, understanding life as the ultimate game can transform how you approach each day.

1. The Rules of Life's Game: Understanding the Structure

In any game, rules serve as the guiding framework. They define how the game is played, what's possible, and what's off-limits. In life, however, the rules are often not as clear-cut. There are societal rules, cultural norms, moral guidelines, and personal values that shape how we make decisions, interact with others, and pursue our goals. And sometimes, these rules are conflicting, confusing, or subject to change as we move through different stages of life.

Think of the rules in life as ever-evolving guidelines that you need to learn and master. Sometimes, the rules are visible and rigid, like laws and regulations. Other times, the rules are subtle, such as social etiquette or the unspoken norms within a family or organization. But there's also room for flexibility. Many times, the most successful people aren't the ones who follow all the rules perfectly but those who know when to bend or reinterpret them to their advantage.

Societal Rules and Expectations

From the moment we're born, society begins to impose rules on us. These might be explicit—such as the laws we must obey—or implicit—like the cultural and social norms we are expected to follow. The path society often lays out for us is straightforward: get an education, find a job, settle down, and retire. But not everyone follows this traditional path, and that's where the game becomes interesting.

There are players who defy societal expectations and carve their own path. These are the entrepreneurs, artists, and thinkers who create new ways of living and thinking. They challenge the status quo and, in doing so, often achieve greatness. But defying the rules comes with risks. It's essential to understand which rules are worth challenging and which ones are there to protect you.

For example, societal pressure may push you to follow a specific career path. Maybe you've been told you need a stable job, like becoming a doctor, engineer, or lawyer, to be successful. However, your passion lies elsewhere—in creative arts, in entrepreneurship, or in something unconventional. By following your heart and taking risks, you may find success and fulfillment that wouldn't have been possible had you stuck to society's prescribed path.

Personal Values as Your Own Set of Rules

While societal rules offer a broad framework, your personal values create your individual rulebook. These are the guiding principles that define who you are, what you stand for, and how you want to live your life. Integrity, compassion, honesty, and ambition are just a few examples of values that might shape your decisions.

Living in alignment with your values helps you make difficult decisions and stay true to yourself, especially when external pressures are pulling you in different directions. For example, let's say you value honesty above all else. This means that, even when lying might be the easiest way out of a situation, you'll choose the truth because it aligns with your internal compass.

However, life will test your values. You might find yourself in situations where you have to balance competing values, like loyalty to a friend versus honesty, or ambition versus empathy. The key is to remain conscious of your values and to make decisions that reflect what's most important to you.

Learning to Play Within—and Outside— the Rules

Some people play life like a board game where every rule must be followed to the letter. They live predictably, never straying from the expected path. Others see life more like a game of poker—part strategy, part luck, where bluffing and bending the rules can sometimes lead to success.

Take risks where you can, but also know that breaking certain rules—like ethical or legal ones—can lead to serious consequences. The best players in life know when to follow the rules and when to push against them. They understand that sometimes, success lies in coloring outside the lines, but only when it aligns with their values and long-term goals.

2. Strategizing for Success: Planning Your Moves

No successful game player approaches a challenge without a strategy. In life, your strategy is your blueprint for how to achieve your goals, overcome obstacles, and manage the complexities that arise along the way. Just as in a game, having a strategy doesn't guarantee success, but it increases your chances of making smart moves that lead to positive outcomes.

Your life strategy can encompass everything from your career and finances to your relationships and personal growth. It's about identifying what you want to achieve and figuring out the steps to get there. However, unlike in most games, life is full of uncertainties, so a good strategy is one that's flexible and adaptable.

Crafting a Personal Strategy: Know Thyself

The foundation of any strong life strategy begins with self-awareness. Before you can set meaningful goals or craft a plan, you need to understand your strengths, weaknesses, values, and desires. This means being brutally honest with yourself about what you're good at, where you need improvement, and what truly motivates you.

For instance, if you're someone who thrives in creative environments but struggles with routine, your strategy might involve seeking career opportunities that allow for innovation and flexibility. If you know that financial security is important to you, then your strategy will likely include clear financial planning and saving goals.

Self-awareness also helps you avoid falling into traps. Many people set goals that don't truly align with who they are. They pursue careers that seem prestigious or follow paths that their family or society expects of them, only to find themselves unfulfilled. Knowing yourself helps you create a life strategy that is authentic and fulfilling.

Setting Short-Term and Long-Term Goals

Any effective strategy requires clear, actionable goals. These should be both short-term—what you want to achieve in the next few months or years—and long-term—what you hope to accomplish over the course of your lifetime. Setting goals provides direction and purpose, giving you something to work toward.

When setting goals, it's important to strike a balance between ambition and realism. While it's great to dream big, setting unattainable goals can lead to frustration and burnout. Start by setting smaller, achievable goals that serve as stepping stones toward your larger ambitions.

For example, if your long-term goal is to start your own business, a short-term goal might be to take courses in entrepreneurship, network with people in your industry, or save a certain amount of money to invest in your venture. Each small step gets you closer to your ultimate objective.

The Power of Adaptability: Embracing Change

Even the best-laid plans can go awry. Life is full of unexpected twists and turns, and no strategy can account for everything. That's why adaptability is one of the most important skills you can cultivate in the game of life.

Being adaptable means having the ability to pivot when necessary. It's about recognizing when your original plan isn't working and having the courage to change course. It also means being open to new opportunities, even when they don't align perfectly with your original strategy.

For instance, imagine you've spent years working toward a promotion at your company, only to realize that the job you're aiming for doesn't truly align with your interests. Adaptability means having the willingness to reassess your goals and pursue a new path that better suits your evolving desires.

Remember, life isn't a linear journey. Sometimes, the most successful people are those who embrace change, take risks, and adapt to new circumstances.

3. Navigating Life's Challenges: Levels of Difficulty

In any game, players face increasing levels of difficulty as they progress. The same is true in life. Each stage of life presents its own unique set of challenges, requiring you to develop new skills, adapt to changing circumstances, and push beyond your comfort zone.

Life's challenges can take many forms—career setbacks, personal losses, health issues, financial difficulties, and relationship problems. How you navigate these challenges determines your success in the game of life.

Early Stages: Learning the Basics

The early stages of life are often focused on learning, exploration, and personal development. Think of this as the tutorial phase of the game, where you're learning the rules, developing skills, and figuring out how to play effectively.

During this stage, it's important to embrace a growth mindset. Mistakes are inevitable, but they are also essential to your development. Whether you're navigating school, entering the workforce, or forming relationships, every experience is an opportunity to learn and grow.

One key challenge in this stage is finding your footing. It's easy to get caught up in comparison—measuring your success against others who seem to be ahead in the game. Remember, everyone's journey is different, and your path is unique to you. Focus on building your own foundation and mastering the basics at your own pace.

Mid-Game: Facing Complex Challenges

As you progress in life, the challenges become more complex. You may face career dilemmas, relationship conflicts, or unexpected setbacks that test your resilience. This is where the game starts to get more intense, and your ability to strategize, adapt, and stay focused becomes crucial.

In the mid-game, it's essential to build a support system. Just as in a multiplayer game, where having strong allies can make or break your success, having a network of friends, family, mentors, and colleagues can provide the support, guidance, and encouragement you need to navigate life's challenges.

Another key challenge in this stage is managing competing priorities. As you take on more responsibilities—such as advancing in your career, building a family, or pursuing personal passions—you'll need to develop strong time-management and decision-making skills. Balancing work, relationships, health, and personal growth requires careful planning and the ability to make difficult choices.

Late-Game: Reflecting and Legacy

In the later stages of life, the focus shifts from achievement to reflection and legacy. This is the point where you look back on the game you've played and evaluate the impact you've made. Did you live authentically? Did you pursue your passions? Did you leave a positive mark on the world?

At this stage, the challenges often revolve around finding meaning and purpose. You may face questions about what you want your legacy to be and how you can continue to contribute to the world in a meaningful way. For some, this might involve mentoring others, giving back to the community, or pursuing new creative projects.

The late-game also offers a chance to redefine success. Rather than focusing on external markers of success—such as wealth, status, or accolades—many people in this stage find fulfillment in relationships, personal growth, and inner peace.

4. Winning in Life's Game: Redefining Success

In a traditional game, winning is defined by a clear outcome—whether that's crossing the finish line first, scoring the most points, or defeating an opponent. But in life, success is much more subjective. It's not about achieving one specific goal or outcome; it's about finding fulfillment, meaning, and happiness on your own terms.

Defining Success for Yourself

One of the biggest challenges in life's game is defining what success looks like for you. Society often tries to dictate what success should be—whether it's financial wealth, career advancement, or social status. But true success is deeply personal.

For some, success might be building a thriving career or accumulating wealth. For others, it might be raising a loving family, traveling the world, or creating art. The key is to define success in a way that aligns with your values, passions, and desires.

This requires introspection and self-awareness. Take time to reflect on what truly makes you happy and fulfilled. What are your core values? What are the moments in life that have brought you the most joy? What kind of legacy do you want to leave behind?

The Journey Over the Destination

In the game of life, the journey is just as important—if not more important—than the destination. While it's natural to set goals and work toward achieving them, it's essential to find joy and meaning in the process. After all, life isn't just about reaching the finish line; it's about experiencing every step along the way.

Take time to appreciate the small victories, the lessons learned, and the personal growth that comes with each challenge. When you focus too much on the end goal, you risk missing out on the richness of the present moment.

Embracing Setbacks as Part of the Game

No one wins at life without encountering setbacks. Whether it's a failed relationship, a career disappointment, or a personal struggle, setbacks are an inevitable part of the game. However, it's not the setbacks themselves that define your success—it's how you respond to them.

Successful players in the game of life view setbacks as opportunities for growth. They don't let failure discourage them; instead, they use it as a learning experience to refine their strategies and become stronger. When you embrace setbacks as part of the game, you develop resilience—the ability to bounce back and keep moving forward, no matter what challenges you face.

5. Conclusion: Playing the Game of Life with Heart and Purpose

Life truly is the ultimate game, full of twists, turns, challenges, and rewards. To play it well, you need a strong sense of self-awareness, a clear strategy, and the resilience to overcome obstacles. But more than anything, you need to approach life with heart, purpose, and a sense of joy.

Whether you're striving for success in your career, relationships, or personal growth, remember that life isn't about perfection. It's about playing the game with integrity, staying true to yourself, and finding meaning in both the wins and the losses.

As you navigate life's complexities, keep in mind that the journey is just as important as the destination. Play with purpose, embrace growth, and find joy in both the successes and the setbacks. In the end, the true reward of life's game isn't in winning—it's in living fully, meaningfully, and authentically.

Quote: "Life is a game. Play it well,
play it with heart, and most of all, play it to the end."
– Unknown

Chapter 5

The Game of Life

Life as the Ultimate Game

Life is a lot like a game—a deeply intricate, multifaceted experience that combines strategy, resilience, knowledge, and emotional depth. However, unlike typical games, it doesn't come with a clear set of rules or an obvious path. You must learn as you go, grow through your experiences, and refine your strategies with each new challenge. At times, you may feel like you're winning; other times, like you're struggling to keep up.

The metaphor of life as a game provides an intriguing perspective on how we live. It helps us see that while we may not be able to control all the circumstances that come our way, we have the power to shape our responses, make strategic moves, and find meaning in both the wins and the losses. The goal isn't just about reaching the end successfully but about playing the game in a way that makes your life rich and purposeful.

In this chapter, we'll dive deep into the concept of life as a game, breaking it down into its essential elements—rules, strategies, challenges, and rewards. We'll explore what it takes to play the game well, how to adapt when life throws curveballs, and why the journey is more important than the destination. Whether you're just starting out in adulthood, navigating mid-life, or reflecting in later years, understanding life as the ultimate game can transform how you approach each day.

1. The Rules of Life's Game: Understanding the Structure

In any game, rules serve as the guiding framework. They define how the game is played, what's possible, and what's off-limits. In life, however, the rules are often not as clear-cut. There are societal rules, cultural norms, moral guidelines, and personal values that shape how we make decisions, interact with others, and pursue our goals. And sometimes, these rules are conflicting, confusing, or subject to change as we move through different stages of life.

Think of the rules in life as ever-evolving guidelines that you need to learn and master. Sometimes, the rules are visible and rigid, like laws and regulations. Other times, the rules are subtle, such as social etiquette or the unspoken norms within a family or organization. But there's also room for flexibility. Many times, the most successful people aren't the ones who follow all the rules perfectly but those who know when to bend or reinterpret them to their advantage.

Societal Rules and Expectations

From the moment we're born, society begins to impose rules on us. These might be explicit—such as the laws we must obey—or implicit—like the cultural and social norms we are expected to follow. The path society often lays out for us is straightforward: get an education, find a job, settle down, and retire. But not everyone follows this traditional path, and that's where the game becomes interesting.

There are players who defy societal expectations and carve their own path. These are the entrepreneurs, artists, and thinkers who create new ways of living and thinking. They challenge the status quo and, in doing so, often achieve greatness. But defying the rules comes with risks. It's essential to understand which rules are worth challenging and which ones are there to protect you.

For example, societal pressure may push you to follow a specific career path. Maybe you've been told you need a stable job, like becoming a doctor, engineer, or lawyer, to be successful. However, your passion lies elsewhere—in creative arts, in entrepreneurship, or in something unconventional. By following your heart and taking risks, you may find success and fulfillment that wouldn't have been possible had you stuck to society's prescribed path.

Personal Values as Your Own Set of Rules

While societal rules offer a broad framework, your personal values create your individual rulebook. These are the guiding principles that define who you are, what you stand for, and how you want to live your life. Integrity, compassion, honesty, and ambition are just a few examples of values that might shape your decisions.

Living in alignment with your values helps you make difficult decisions and stay true to yourself, especially when external pressures are pulling you in different directions. For example, let's say you value honesty above all else. This means that, even when lying might be the easiest way out of a situation, you'll choose the truth because it aligns with your internal compass.

However, life will test your values. You might find yourself in situations where you have to balance competing values, like loyalty to a friend versus honesty, or ambition versus empathy. The key is to remain conscious of your values and to make decisions that reflect what's most important to you.

Learning to Play Within—and Outside— the Rules

Some people play life like a board game where every rule must be followed to the letter. They live predictably, never straying from the expected path. Others see life more like a game of poker—part strategy, part luck, where bluffing and bending the rules can sometimes lead to success.

Take risks where you can, but also know that breaking certain rules—like ethical or legal ones—can lead to serious consequences. The best players in life know when to follow the rules and when to push against them. They understand that sometimes, success lies in coloring outside the lines, but only when it aligns with their values and long-term goals.

2. Strategizing for Success: Planning Your Moves

No successful game player approaches a challenge without a strategy. In life, your strategy is your blueprint for how to achieve your goals, overcome obstacles, and manage the complexities that arise along the way. Just as in a game, having a strategy doesn't guarantee success, but it increases your chances of making smart moves that lead to positive outcomes.

Your life strategy can encompass everything from your career and finances to your relationships and personal growth. It's about identifying what you want to achieve and figuring out the steps to get there. However, unlike in most games, life is full of uncertainties, so a good strategy is one that's flexible and adaptable.

Crafting a Personal Strategy: Know Thyself

The foundation of any strong life strategy begins with self-awareness. Before you can set meaningful goals or craft a plan, you need to understand your strengths, weaknesses, values, and desires. This means being brutally honest with yourself about what you're good at, where you need improvement, and what truly motivates you.

For instance, if you're someone who thrives in creative environments but struggles with routine, your strategy might involve seeking career opportunities that allow for innovation and flexibility. If you know that financial security is important to you, then your strategy will likely include clear financial planning and saving goals.

Self-awareness also helps you avoid falling into traps. Many people set goals that don't truly align with who they are. They pursue careers that seem prestigious or follow paths that their family or society expects of them, only to find themselves unfulfilled. Knowing yourself helps you create a life strategy that is authentic and fulfilling.

Setting Short-Term and Long-Term Goals

Any effective strategy requires clear, actionable goals. These should be both short-term—what you want to achieve in the next few months or years—and long-term—what you hope to accomplish over the course of your lifetime. Setting goals provides direction and purpose, giving you something to work toward.

When setting goals, it's important to strike a balance between ambition and realism. While it's great to dream big, setting unattainable goals can lead to frustration and burnout. Start by setting smaller, achievable goals that serve as stepping stones toward your larger ambitions.

For example, if your long-term goal is to start your own business, a short-term goal might be to take courses in entrepreneurship, network with people in your industry, or save a certain amount of money to invest in your venture. Each small step gets you closer to your ultimate objective.

The Power of Adaptability: Embracing Change

Even the best-laid plans can go awry. Life is full of unexpected twists and turns, and no strategy can account for everything. That's why adaptability is one of the most important skills you can cultivate in the game of life.

Being adaptable means having the ability to pivot when necessary. It's about recognizing when your original plan isn't working and having the courage to change course. It also means being open to new opportunities, even when they don't align perfectly with your original strategy.

For instance, imagine you've spent years working toward a promotion at your company, only to realize that the job you're aiming for doesn't truly align with your interests. Adaptability means having the willingness to reassess your goals and pursue a new path that better suits your evolving desires.

Remember, life isn't a linear journey. Sometimes, the most successful people are those who embrace change, take risks, and adapt to new circumstances.

3. Navigating Life's Challenges: Levels of Difficulty

In any game, players face increasing levels of difficulty as they progress. The same is true in life. Each stage of life presents its own unique set of challenges, requiring you to develop new skills, adapt to changing circumstances, and push beyond your comfort zone.

Life's challenges can take many forms—career setbacks, personal losses, health issues, financial difficulties, and relationship problems. How you navigate these challenges determines your success in the game of life.

Early Stages: Learning the Basics

The early stages of life are often focused on learning, exploration, and personal development. Think of this as the tutorial phase of the game, where you're learning the rules, developing skills, and figuring out how to play effectively.

During this stage, it's important to embrace a growth mindset. Mistakes are inevitable, but they are also essential to your development. Whether you're navigating school, entering the workforce, or forming relationships, every experience is an opportunity to learn and grow.

One key challenge in this stage is finding your footing. It's easy to get caught up in comparison—measuring your success against others who seem to be ahead in the game. Remember, everyone's journey is different, and your path is unique to you. Focus on building your own foundation and mastering the basics at your own pace.

Mid-Game: Facing Complex Challenges

As you progress in life, the challenges become more complex. You may face career dilemmas, relationship conflicts, or unexpected setbacks that test your resilience. This is where the game starts to get more intense, and your ability to strategize, adapt, and stay focused becomes crucial.

In the mid-game, it's essential to build a support system. Just as in a multiplayer game, where having strong allies can make or break your success, having a network of friends, family, mentors, and colleagues can provide the support, guidance, and encouragement you need to navigate life's challenges.

Another key challenge in this stage is managing competing priorities. As you take on more responsibilities—such as advancing in your career, building a family, or pursuing personal passions—you'll need to develop strong time-management and decision-making skills. Balancing work, relationships, health, and personal growth requires careful planning and the ability to make difficult choices.

Late-Game: Reflecting and Legacy

In the later stages of life, the focus shifts from achievement to reflection and legacy. This is the point where you look back on the game you've played and evaluate the impact you've made. Did you live authentically? Did you pursue your passions? Did you leave a positive mark on the world?

At this stage, the challenges often revolve around finding meaning and purpose. You may face questions about what you want your legacy to be and how you can continue to contribute to the world in a meaningful way. For some, this might involve mentoring others, giving back to the community, or pursuing new creative projects.

The late-game also offers a chance to redefine success. Rather than focusing on external markers of success—such as wealth, status, or accolades—many people in this stage find fulfillment in relationships, personal growth, and inner peace.

4. Winning in Life's Game: Redefining Success

In a traditional game, winning is defined by a clear outcome—whether that's crossing the finish line first, scoring the most points, or defeating an opponent. But in life, success is much more subjective. It's not about achieving one specific goal or outcome; it's about finding fulfillment, meaning, and happiness on your own terms.

Defining Success for Yourself

One of the biggest challenges in life's game is defining what success looks like for you. Society often tries to dictate what success should be—whether it's financial wealth, career advancement, or social status. But true success is deeply personal.

For some, success might be building a thriving career or accumulating wealth. For others, it might be raising a loving family, traveling the world, or creating art. The key is to define success in a way that aligns with your values, passions, and desires.

This requires introspection and self-awareness. Take time to reflect on what truly makes you happy and fulfilled. What are your core values? What are the moments in life that have brought you the most joy? What kind of legacy do you want to leave behind?

The Journey Over the Destination

In the game of life, the journey is just as important—if not more important—than the destination. While it's natural to set goals and work toward achieving them, it's essential to find joy and meaning in the process. After all, life isn't just about reaching the finish line; it's about experiencing every step along the way.

Take time to appreciate the small victories, the lessons learned, and the personal growth that comes with each challenge. When you focus too much on the end goal, you risk missing out on the richness of the present moment.

Embracing Setbacks as Part of the Game

No one wins at life without encountering setbacks. Whether it's a failed relationship, a career disappointment, or a personal struggle, setbacks are an inevitable part of the game. However, it's not the setbacks themselves that define your success—it's how you respond to them.

Successful players in the game of life view setbacks as opportunities for growth. They don't let failure discourage them; instead, they use it as a learning experience to refine their strategies and become stronger. When you embrace setbacks as part of the game, you develop resilience—the ability to bounce back and keep moving forward, no matter what challenges you face.

5. Conclusion: Playing the Game of Life with Heart and Purpose

Life truly is the ultimate game, full of twists, turns, challenges, and rewards. To play it well, you need a strong sense of self-awareness, a clear strategy, and the resilience to overcome obstacles. But more than anything, you need to approach life with heart, purpose, and a sense of joy.

Whether you're striving for success in your career, relationships, or personal growth, remember that life isn't about perfection. It's about playing the game with integrity, staying true to yourself, and finding meaning in both the wins and the losses.

As you navigate life's complexities, keep in mind that the journey is just as important as the destination. Play with purpose, embrace growth, and find joy in both the successes and the setbacks. In the end, the true reward of life's game isn't in winning—it's in living fully, meaningfully, and authentically.

"Life is a game. Play it well, play it with heart, and most of all, play it to the end."

The Power of Emotional Intelligence in Life's Game

In the game of life, it's easy to believe that intellect, skills, or sheer determination are the key ingredients for success. However, one of the most overlooked yet crucial elements is emotional intelligence (EI). Emotional intelligence isn't just about managing your emotions—it's about understanding yourself and others on a deeper level, fostering meaningful relationships, and navigating the complex emotional landscapes that define human interactions.

Life is not just a collection of tasks to complete or obstacles to overcome. It's about the connections you make, the empathy you show, and the emotions you experience. Whether you're striving to achieve personal goals, building professional success, or fostering strong relationships, emotional intelligence can elevate your life to a new level of fulfillment and success. It is, in many ways, the secret weapon to mastering life's game.

This chapter delves into the various aspects of emotional intelligence and how mastering it can change the way you approach life's challenges and opportunities. By developing EI, you can improve your relationships, decision-making, and overall sense of well-being.

1. Understanding Emotional Intelligence: The Foundation

Emotional intelligence is the ability to recognize, understand, manage, and influence both your own emotions and the emotions of others. It's made up of several core components: self-awareness, self-regulation, empathy, social skills, and motivation. Together, these elements form the foundation of how you interact with the world on an emotional level.

Self-Awareness: Knowing Yourself

Self-awareness is the cornerstone of emotional intelligence. It involves being in tune with your emotions, knowing how they affect your thoughts and behavior, and recognizing your strengths and weaknesses. When you're self-aware, you can better understand why you react to certain situations the way you do, allowing you to make conscious decisions about how to handle those situations.

For example, let's say you're in a high-pressure situation at work. Without self-awareness, you might react impulsively—perhaps snapping at a colleague or making a rash decision. But if you're aware of your emotions, you can take a step back, recognize that you're feeling stressed, and choose a more thoughtful response. Self-awareness gives you the power to control your emotions instead of letting them control you.

Self-awareness also extends to understanding your triggers—those situations or people that push your buttons. Once you know what triggers you, you can prepare yourself to manage your reactions more effectively.

Self-Regulation: Mastering Your Emotions

Once you've developed self-awareness, the next step is self-regulation. This is the ability to control your emotions and reactions in a healthy and productive way. Self-regulation doesn't mean suppressing your emotions, but rather understanding them and choosing how to express them.

Imagine you're in a heated argument with a loved one. Your first instinct might be to raise your voice or say something hurtful. But self-regulation allows you to pause, take a deep breath, and respond calmly instead. It's about choosing not to act out of anger or frustration, but rather responding in a way that aligns with your values and long-term goals.

Self-regulation also plays a crucial role in managing stress. Life is full of stressful moments, but those who have mastered self-regulation can remain calm under pressure and make better decisions, even in difficult circumstances.

Empathy: Understanding Others

Empathy is the ability to put yourself in someone else's shoes and understand their emotions. It's about being able to connect with others on an emotional level, which is essential for building strong relationships—whether personal or professional.

When you're empathetic, you can see beyond your own perspective and truly understand what someone else is feeling. This can help you navigate conflicts, build rapport, and offer support when others need it most. In the workplace, empathy allows you to be a better leader or team member by fostering collaboration and trust.

Empathy doesn't mean you always have to agree with others, but it does mean that you respect their emotions and are willing to listen. This can defuse tense situations and lead to more productive, meaningful interactions.

Social Skills: Building Connections

Social skills are the tools you use to interact with others effectively. These include communication, teamwork, conflict resolution, and leadership abilities. Strong social skills enable you to build and maintain relationships, whether at work or in your personal life.

Effective communication is at the heart of social skills. This isn't just about talking but about listening—really hearing what the other person is saying and responding in a way that fosters connection. Strong communicators can articulate their thoughts and feelings clearly while also being open to others' perspectives.

In life's game, your ability to build relationships and work with others is a major factor in your success. People with strong social skills are often seen as more likable and trustworthy, which can open doors both personally and professionally.

Motivation: The Drive to Succeed

Motivation, in the context of emotional intelligence, refers to the internal drive to pursue goals with energy and persistence. People with high emotional intelligence are often self-motivated; they have a clear sense of purpose and are driven by their internal values rather than external rewards like money or status.

When you're motivated, setbacks don't discourage you—instead, they fuel your determination to keep pushing forward. Emotional intelligence helps you stay focused on your long-term goals, even when the path becomes difficult. It's about having the resilience to overcome obstacles and the passion to continue learning and growing.

2. The Role of Emotional Intelligence in Personal Relationships

Emotional intelligence is the key to building and maintaining strong, healthy relationships. Whether it's a romantic relationship, a friendship, or a family bond, the ability to understand and manage emotions is critical to fostering connection and trust.

Conflict Resolution: Navigating Emotional Turbulence

Conflict is inevitable in any relationship. What sets emotionally intelligent people apart is their ability to navigate conflict in a way that strengthens, rather than weakens, their relationships. When emotions are running high, it's easy to react impulsively or say something hurtful. But those with high emotional intelligence can step back, manage their emotions, and approach the situation calmly and thoughtfully.

In a romantic relationship, for example, emotional intelligence allows you to communicate openly with your partner about your feelings without becoming defensive or aggressive. This helps you resolve conflicts in a way that brings you closer together, rather than driving a wedge between you.

Emotional Support: Being There for Others

One of the most powerful aspects of emotional intelligence is the ability to offer emotional support to those around you. Whether it's a friend going through a tough time or a partner facing a challenge, your ability to empathize and provide support can make all the difference.

Offering emotional support isn't just about listening—it's about being fully present for the other person, validating their feelings, and offering comfort. When you can provide this kind of support, you strengthen the bond between you and the other person, creating a foundation of trust and intimacy.

Building Emotional Intimacy

In romantic relationships, emotional intelligence is key to building emotional intimacy. Emotional intimacy is the deep sense of closeness and connection that comes from truly understanding and being understood by your partner. It's about being open, vulnerable, and authentic with each other.

When both partners have high emotional intelligence, they can communicate their needs and desires more effectively, navigate challenges together, and build a relationship that is both fulfilling and resilient. Emotional intimacy is what transforms a good relationship into a great one.

3. Emotional Intelligence in Professional Success

While emotional intelligence is often associated with personal relationships, it's just as important in the professional world. In fact, research has shown that emotional intelligence is one of the strongest predictors of workplace success.

Leadership and Emotional Intelligence

Great leaders aren't just intelligent or skilled—they have high emotional intelligence. They know how to motivate their teams, handle stress, and create an environment of trust and respect. Leaders with emotional intelligence are able to connect with their employees on a personal level, which fosters loyalty and engagement.

For example, a manager with high emotional intelligence will recognize when a team member is struggling and offer support, whether that's through mentoring, providing resources, or simply offering a listening ear. This not only helps the employee but also creates a positive, productive work environment.

Teamwork and Collaboration

In the workplace, emotional intelligence is essential for effective teamwork and collaboration. When people are in tune with their emotions and the emotions of others, they can work together more smoothly, resolve conflicts more easily, and achieve better outcomes.

For instance, in a group project, emotional intelligence allows team members to communicate openly, respect each other's perspectives, and manage any tensions that arise. This leads to more creative problem-solving and better results overall.

Managing Stress and Pressure

Work can be stressful, especially when deadlines are tight or projects are complex. Emotional intelligence helps you manage that stress in a healthy way, so it doesn't interfere with your performance or well-being.

When you can recognize your stress triggers and develop strategies to manage them—such as taking breaks, practicing mindfulness, or seeking support—you'll be better equipped to stay focused and productive under pressure.

4. Developing Emotional Intelligence: Practical Steps

Emotional intelligence isn't something you're born with—it's a skill that can be developed over time with practice and self-reflection. Here are some practical steps to enhance your emotional intelligence:

Practice Self-Reflection

Take time each day to reflect on your emotions and how they affect your thoughts and actions. Ask yourself: How did I handle that situation? What emotions was I feeling? What could I have done differently? Self-reflection helps you become more aware of your emotional patterns and how they influence your behavior.

Seek Feedback

One of the best ways to improve your emotional intelligence is to seek feedback from others. Ask trusted friends, family members, or colleagues for their honest opinions about how you handle emotions and relationships. This can provide valuable insights into areas where you can improve.

Develop Mindfulness

Mindfulness is the practice of being fully present in the moment, without judgment. By developing mindfulness, you can become more aware of your emotions and how they affect your thoughts and behavior. This can help you manage stress, improve focus, and enhance your relationships.

Practice Empathy

Make a conscious effort to put yourself in others' shoes and understand their emotions. This can be as simple as asking someone how they're feeling or imagining how you would feel in their situation. The more you practice empathy, the better you'll become at connecting with others on an emotional level.

5. Conclusion: Mastering Life's Game with Emotional Intelligence

Emotional intelligence is one of the most powerful tools you can develop to master the game of life. It enhances your relationships, improves your decision-making, and helps you navigate the emotional complexities of life with grace and resilience. By developing self-awareness, self-regulation, empathy, social skills, and motivation, you'll be better equipped to handle whatever challenges life throws your way.

Ultimately, emotional intelligence allows you to live a more fulfilling, connected, and successful life—both personally and professionally. It's not just about winning the game—it's about playing it with heart, purpose, and understanding.

Creating Your Own Rules

Life is a complex web of expectations, societal norms, traditions, and unwritten codes that seem to shape our every move. From a young age, we are taught what is "acceptable" and "normal." But the ultimate game-changer in life is not following those norms blindly but learning to craft your own rules. When you create your own rules, you claim the power to dictate your life, making choices based on your values, desires, and ambitions.

Creating personal rules doesn't mean breaking every societal norm; rather, it is about understanding who you are, what you value, and how to live authentically while balancing the expectations of the outside world. This chapter dives deep into the art of self-discovery, the process of introspection, and how you can build your own set of personal guidelines that align with your core values and goals.

1. The Importance of Introspection and Self-Awareness

The foundation of creating your own rules is self-awareness. Before we can set meaningful boundaries, principles, and goals, we need to know who we are, what we stand for, and what we want from life.

The Power of Knowing Yourself

Knowing yourself sounds simple, but it's one of the most challenging yet rewarding journeys one can undertake. Many people go through life not fully aware of their deepest motivations, passions, and emotions. Introspection is an ongoing process that requires patience, honesty, and vulnerability. When you know yourself, you can make better decisions, avoid manipulative situations, and live in a way that feels right to you.

Reflection Exercise:

Take some time each day to sit with your thoughts. Whether it's through journaling or simply being still, asking yourself the following questions can help deepen your understanding of yourself:

- What makes me happy, and what makes me frustrated?

- When was the last time I felt truly passionate or alive?

- What are my non-negotiables—things I absolutely need in my life?

Story of Self-Awareness:

One striking example of someone who transformed their life through self-awareness is Steve Jobs. Known for his innovative thinking and creative genius, Jobs didn't always fit into the traditional norms of success. After dropping out of college and exploring different paths, he spent time in India, studied Zen Buddhism, and delved deeply into philosophy and spirituality. It was during this time that he gained clarity about his vision for Apple, which would later revolutionize the tech world.

Jobs' story illustrates the importance of deep introspection and how knowing oneself can shape a clearer vision for the future. His rule? Think differently. He embraced his unconventional nature and turned it into one of the most successful guiding principles in modern business.

2. Techniques for Discovering Your True Self

Understanding yourself goes far beyond casual introspection. There are structured ways to dig deeper into your identity and uncover who you truly are. These include various methods, such as journaling, meditation, exploration, and seeking feedback.

1. Journaling

Journaling is one of the most powerful tools for self-discovery. When you put your thoughts and feelings on paper, you allow your subconscious mind to express itself. This uncensored version of your inner thoughts can reveal patterns, desires, and fears that you may not have consciously noticed.

Technique: Start a daily journaling habit by writing down your thoughts, fears, accomplishments, and dreams. Over time, reflect on your entries to identify recurring themes. These themes can give you insight into your true passions and values.

> *"Journaling is like whispering to one's self and listening at the same time." – Mina Murray.*

2. Meditation

Meditation encourages mindfulness, a practice of staying present in the moment and observing your thoughts without judgment. Through regular meditation, you can begin to understand your thought patterns and emotional triggers, leading to greater self-awareness.

Technique: Dedicate 10-20 minutes a day to mindfulness meditation. Focus on your breath and allow thoughts to come and go without engaging with them. This practice will teach you to observe your emotions and feelings more objectively.

3. Exploration and Travel

Often, we discover our true selves not by looking inward but by stepping outside our comfort zones. Travel is a potent tool for self-discovery because it exposes us to different cultures, people, and experiences that challenge our assumptions about life.

Set a goal to travel solo or engage in an activity that pushes you out of your normal routine. Whether it's a hiking trip, a solo vacation to a foreign country, or enrolling in a completely new class, exploration helps reveal parts of yourself that are hidden beneath the surface.

Cheryl Strayed, author of *Wild*, found clarity after embarking on a solo hiking journey through the Pacific Crest Trail. Through her journey, she realized her capacity for resilience, independence, and healing.

4. Seeking Feedback

While introspection is valuable, feedback from others can provide insights that you might overlook. Trusted friends or mentors can offer perspectives on your behavior and personality that can reveal blind spots or patterns you've missed.

Ask a few close friends or colleagues for honest feedback on your strengths, weaknesses, and tendencies. Use their insights as a mirror to further explore your true self.

"We all need people who will give us feedback. That's how we improve." – Bill Gates

3. Stepping Outside Societal Norms to Find Clarity

Society often imposes expectations on us. These norms dictate how we should behave, what we should strive for, and even how we should look or feel. While societal rules can provide structure, they can also stifle individuality. Stepping outside these norms is crucial for discovering your true self and crafting your unique set of rules.

1. Challenging Societal Expectations

Many of us grow up with a predefined script handed to us by our families, schools, or society at large. We're told to follow a specific path: get an education, find a stable job, marry, buy a house, and start a family. While these milestones may resonate with some, they don't align with everyone's dreams or values.

Reflect on your current path. Are you following it because it's what you truly want, or are you adhering to it because it's expected of you? If you discover that societal expectations are shaping your life choices, consider ways to break free and pursue what feels authentic.

A woman named Emily always felt pressured to become a doctor because it was what her parents wanted. However, after completing medical school, she realized that her true passion was in art. Stepping outside societal expectations, she left her medical career behind and pursued art full-time. Today, she's a renowned artist who finds immense joy and fulfillment in her work.

"The greatest challenge in life is discovering who you are. The second greatest is being happy with what you find." – Auliq Ice.

2. The Courage to Forge Your Own Path

It takes immense courage to step away from the life that's expected of you and forge your own path. Fear of judgment, failure, and uncertainty can make this process daunting, but the rewards of living authentically far outweigh the risks.

Richard Branson, founder of the Virgin Group, exemplifies someone who followed his own path despite societal skepticism. Branson dropped out of high school and faced numerous failures in his early business ventures. Yet, his refusal to conform to traditional rules allowed him to build an empire based on innovation and audacity.

Take small steps toward independence by questioning one societal norm that doesn't resonate with you. For instance, if you feel pressured to work a 9-to-5 job but crave flexibility, explore freelance opportunities or remote work options.

4. Crafting Your Own Rules

After gaining clarity through self-awareness and exploration, the next crucial step is to craft your own personal rules. These rules are meant to serve as your guide, helping you navigate life's choices, set boundaries, and stay aligned with your purpose. When built upon your core values, they ensure that the life you live is authentic and fulfilling.

1. Identify Your Core Values

To craft meaningful rules, it's essential to start with your core values. These are the guiding principles that shape the way you approach life. They influence everything from your decisions to your goals, relationships, and how you spend your time. Understanding and defining these values is the foundation upon which your personal rules are built.

Start by asking yourself: What truly matters to me? What are the non-negotiable principles in my life? From here, write down your top five core values—these may include values such as honesty, independence, kindness, creativity, or adventure. Once you've listed them, think about how they influence your daily life and what actions you can take to prioritize them.

> *"Your values are the foundation of your rules. When you align your actions with your values, you create a life that feels authentic and meaningful."*

2. Create Clear Boundaries

Personal rules are about more than just values—they're also about setting boundaries that protect your emotional, physical, and mental well-being. Boundaries are essential in relationships, work, and everyday life. When you establish clear boundaries, you communicate your limits, ensuring that others understand what is acceptable and what is not.

For example, if your core value is self-respect, a personal rule could be to never allow someone to disrespect you or take advantage of your kindness. This might mean walking away from toxic friendships, relationships, or workplaces where your boundaries are not honored.

Setting boundaries might feel difficult at first, but they are key to maintaining healthy relationships and protecting your peace of mind. Think of boundaries as the walls that keep you grounded, helping you navigate the world while protecting your integrity.

"Boundaries are a form of self-love. They protect your space and energy, allowing you to live life on your terms."

3. Define What Success Looks Like for You

Another important step in crafting your personal rules is defining what success means to you. Society often places pressure on us to achieve certain milestones—whether it's career success, financial wealth, or social status—but real success is deeply personal. It should align with your values, passions, and life goals.

Take the time to reflect on what success truly means to you. Is it finding balance in your life? Is it building meaningful relationships? Or is it living a life filled with creativity and purpose? Once you define success on your own terms, you can create rules that guide you toward that vision.

For instance, if balance is important to you, a personal rule could be to ensure you make time for your passions, family, and well-being, regardless of how busy life gets. By following this rule, you're creating a life that feels fulfilling, rather than chasing an external definition of success.

"True success is living according to your own values, not someone else's expectations."

4. Prioritize Self-Care

Self-care is a fundamental part of maintaining a healthy and fulfilling life. Crafting personal rules around self-care ensures that you remain physically, mentally, and emotionally strong enough to pursue your goals and live in alignment with your values. It's easy to get caught up in life's demands, but without proper self-care, burnout becomes inevitable.

For examample, if mental health is one of your core values, a personal rule could be to dedicate time each day for relaxation, whether that's through meditation, exercise, journaling, or simply taking a break. Self-care also involves saying no to situations, people, or responsibilities that drain your energy.

"Self-care is not selfish; it's a way to ensure that you can give your best self to everything you do."

5. Embrace Flexibility

While your core values may stay constant, your personal rules don't have to be rigid. Life is full of changes and new experiences, and it's important to stay adaptable. Embracing flexibility in your rules allows you to grow and evolve while still staying aligned with your values.

For example, if you value adventure and one of your personal rules involves being spontaneous and seeking new experiences, you may need to adjust your rule as you grow older or as life circumstances change. The key is to allow your rules to reflect your current reality while staying true to your values.

Flexibility doesn't mean abandoning your principles—it means being open to adjusting your approach when necessary, without losing sight of what's important to you.

"Life is fluid, and so should your rules be. Staying adaptable allows you to grow while staying aligned with your values."

6. Accountability and Reflection

Once you've established your personal rules, it's important to hold yourself accountable. Regularly reflect on whether you are living according to your values and the rules you've set for yourself. This might involve journaling, talking with a trusted friend, or even setting goals that align with your personal guidelines.

If you find that you've strayed from your rules or that they no longer serve you, it's okay to reassess. Personal growth is a continuous process, and sometimes that means tweaking your rules to reflect new insights or life circumstances.

"Accountability isn't about perfection; it's about progress. Reflect on your actions and align them with the life you want to create."

7. Living Authentically

Ultimately, personal rules are about living authentically and true to yourself. In a world where it's easy to get lost in the noise of societal expectations, your rules help keep you grounded. They serve as a guidepost, ensuring that your actions and decisions reflect your true self, not what others expect of you.

When you live authentically, you create a sense of fulfillment and peace. You are no longer chasing external validation, but instead, are living according to what feels right for you. Your life becomes a reflection of your values, and your rules are the map that keeps you aligned with your purpose.

> *"To live authentically is to create a life that mirrors your values and desires, rather than someone else's expectations."*

By identifying your core values, setting boundaries, defining success, prioritizing self-care, embracing flexibility, holding yourself accountable, and living authentically, you can craft personal rules that guide you toward a life that feels meaningful, balanced, and true to who you are. These rules are not set in stone but evolve with you as you grow and learn, ensuring that you remain aligned with your core values and purpose throughout your life.

5. Implementing Your Rules in Everyday Life

Creating your own rules is a monumental step, but the real challenge lies in implementing those rules consistently. Life is full of distractions, societal pressures, and conflicting desires that can tempt you to stray from your personal principles. Staying true to your values while navigating everyday life is key to living authentically.

1. Small, Consistent Actions

One of the most effective ways to implement your rules is by focusing on small, consistent actions that align with your core values. Big, sweeping changes are difficult to maintain, but small steps—when practiced regularly—can lead to powerful transformations over time.

If one of your rules is to prioritize creativity, set aside 30 minutes each day to engage in a creative activity. Whether it's painting, writing, or brainstorming new ideas, the key is to consistently carve out time for it in your schedule.

James Clear, author of *Atomic Habits*, advocates for the power of small habits. He highlights how small, consistent changes can compound into significant life shifts. His philosophy aligns with the idea that small, actionable steps are easier to maintain and more effective in the long run.

> *"Success is the product of daily habits—not once-in-a-lifetime transformations." – James Clear.*

2. Accountability Systems

Holding yourself accountable is crucial for staying on track with your personal rules. Without accountability, it's easy to become complacent or fall back into old habits. Accountability can come in the form of self-monitoring, seeking support from others, or even technology.

Consider using an app that tracks your progress or keeps you motivated. There are apps for fitness, mindfulness, and even creativity that can help you monitor your progress and ensure you're sticking to your rules.

Tim Ferriss, author of *The 4-Hour Workweek*, often emphasizes the power of accountability systems. Ferriss himself has implemented various productivity hacks—such as using public commitments and personal tracking systems—to ensure that he stays true to his personal goals.

> *"You are the average of the five people you spend the most time with." – Jim Rohn.*

Surround yourself with people who will hold you accountable for living your values.

3. Adapting to Challenges and Setbacks

No matter how carefully you craft your personal rules, life will inevitably throw challenges and setbacks your way. What's important is how you respond to these obstacles. Adaptability is key to maintaining your personal rules without becoming rigid or inflexible.

Understanding Flexibility:

Some people believe that creating personal rules requires rigid discipline. However, true strength lies in flexibility—knowing when to adjust your rules to new circumstances while still staying true to your core values. For example, if your rule is to never compromise your integrity, you might still find ways to navigate difficult ethical decisions that preserve both your values and practicality.

Oprah Winfrey is known for her adaptability in the face of challenges. She's shared stories about how she had to adjust her goals and vision many times throughout her career. Despite setbacks, she always stayed true to her core belief in the power of storytelling and giving a voice to the voiceless.

When faced with a challenge, ask yourself: "How can I stay true to my values while adapting to this new reality?" Flexibility is about bending without breaking, finding creative solutions that align with your long-term goals.

"Adaptability is not imitation. It means power of resistance and assimilation." – Mahatma Gandhi.

6. The Role of Discipline and Commitment in Personal Rule-Making

Creating your own rules involves more than self-awareness and discovery; it also requires a strong sense of discipline and commitment. Without these, even the most well-intentioned rules can falter.

1. Building Self-Discipline

Self-discipline is the backbone of following through with your personal rules. It's easy to create rules in moments of clarity and inspiration, but the real challenge comes when temptation or distractions arise. Building self-discipline helps you stay focused and avoid the pitfalls of complacency.

Techniques for Building Discipline:

- **Start small**: Begin by committing to small, manageable actions rather than overwhelming yourself with too many changes at once.

- **Practice delayed gratification**: Strengthen your willpower by practicing small acts of delayed gratification—whether that's waiting an extra 10 minutes before indulging in a treat or resisting the urge to check your phone constantly.

- **Reward progress**: Celebrate your small victories along the way to build momentum and encourage long-term discipline.

> *"Discipline is the bridge between goals and accomplishment." – Jim Rohn.*

2. The Power of Commitment

While discipline helps you manage your daily actions, commitment is what keeps you grounded in the long-term. Commitment means sticking to your rules and goals even when the path becomes difficult or unclear.

Story of Commitment:

One powerful story of commitment comes from J.K. Rowling. Before becoming a household name with the *Harry Potter* series, Rowling faced multiple rejections from publishers, struggled with depression, and lived as a single mother on welfare. However, her commitment to her vision kept her writing and eventually led her to global success. Rowling's ability to stay true to her rule—to never give up on her dream—was key to her triumph.

Write down your top three life goals and then write a short statement for each one about why you're committed to achieving it. Reflect on these statements regularly to remind yourself of your dedication.

"When you are committed to something, you accept no excuses—only results." – Ken Blanchard.

7. Stories of Rule-Breakers Who Changed the World

Throughout history, there have been individuals who defied the norms of their time, rejecting the rules imposed upon them and choosing to live by their own. These pioneers serve as powerful reminders that great change often comes when we follow our own path, even when it means breaking the mold set by society. Their stories inspire us to reflect on our own lives and consider whether the rules we follow truly align with our values.

1. Steve Jobs: Redefining Innovation and Creativity

Steve Jobs, co-founder of Apple, revolutionized technology and design by refusing to accept limitations. He famously ignored conventional wisdom about what a personal computer should be, constantly challenging the status quo in pursuit of innovation. His rule was simple: *Think differently*. Jobs broke away from traditional corporate structures and embraced his vision of blending technology with design to create user-friendly products. Despite facing criticism and even being ousted from his own company, Jobs remained true to his principles, ultimately returning to Apple to introduce revolutionary products like the iPhone, iPod, and MacBook, which forever changed the tech landscape.

Jobs' life teaches us that challenging the status quo, pushing boundaries, and believing in one's vision—no matter how unconventional—can lead to transformative success.

> *"Here's to the crazy ones, the misfits, the rebels, the troublemakers… because the ones who are crazy enough to think they can change the world, are the ones who do."*
> *— Steve Jobs.*

2. Rosa Parks: Standing Against Injustice

Rosa Parks, known as "the mother of the civil rights movement," made history by refusing to give up her seat to a white man on a segregated bus in Montgomery, Alabama, in 1955. Her rule-breaking act of defiance became a symbol of the fight against racial injustice in the United States. At the time, segregation laws dictated that African Americans had to sit at the back of the bus and give up their seats for white passengers. Parks, tired of the oppression and discrimination, chose to stand her ground, sparking the Montgomery Bus Boycott and playing a pivotal role in the civil rights movement.

Parks' simple but courageous action reminds us that standing up for what's right—even when it's against the law—can lead to profound societal change.

"I would like to be remembered as a person who wanted to be free... so other people would be also free."
– Rosa Parks.

3. Bruce Lee: Breaking Cultural and Physical Barriers

Bruce Lee wasn't just a martial artist; he was a philosopher, actor, and cultural icon who broke numerous barriers throughout his career. Born in the United States but raised in Hong Kong, Lee defied the stereotypes and limitations that Asian actors faced in Hollywood. He introduced martial arts to Western cinema, forever altering the film industry and popular culture. Lee's personal philosophy, *Jeet Kune Do* (The Way of the Intercepting Fist), emphasized fluidity and adaptability rather than strict adherence to tradition—reflecting his belief in breaking away from rigid norms.

Lee's refusal to be boxed in by cultural expectations or physical limitations inspired millions, showing that self-expression and the breaking of boundaries can create lasting impact.

"Absorb what is useful, discard what is not, add what is uniquely your own." – Bruce Lee.

8. The Ongoing Process of Rule-Creation

Creating your own rules is not a one-time process. As you grow and evolve, your rules may need to be adjusted to fit new circumstances, experiences, and desires. Being open to change and allowing yourself to adapt your rules over time is essential for continued growth.

1. Revisiting and Reevaluating Your Rules

It's important to periodically reflect on your rules and assess whether they still serve you. As you progress through different stages of life, your values may shift, and the rules you created in the past may no longer align with who you are today.

Set aside time every six months to reflect on your rules. Ask yourself: Are these rules still serving me? If not, what adjustments need to be made?

"Don't be afraid to change the rules if they no longer fit the game you're playing."

2. Allowing Room for Growth

Personal growth is a continuous journey. By allowing yourself room to grow and evolve, you'll be better equipped to handle life's changes while staying true to your core values.

Nelson Mandela's life is a perfect example of someone who allowed room for growth and transformation. From a militant activist to a champion of peace and reconciliation, Mandela adapted his personal rules to fit the changing needs of his country and people. HIs rule to prioritize unity over vengeance became the cornerstone of his leadership during South Africa's transition from apartheid to democracy.

Conclusion: Crafting a Life of Authenticity

Creating your own rules is the ultimate act of self-empowerment. It's a commitment to live life on your terms, to stay true to your values, and to forge a path that is uniquely your own. The process of self-discovery, reflection, and growth is ongoing, but each step you take brings you closer to living a life that feels authentic and meaningful.

By understanding yourself, challenging societal norms, and crafting personal guidelines that reflect your deepest desires and beliefs, you can play the game of life in a way that truly resonates with who you are.